THE ZEN OF HOME WATER

TRUE TALES OF ADVENTURE, TRAVEL, AND FLY FISHING

JERRY HAMZA

Skyhorse Publishing

Skyhorse Publishing books may be purchased in bulk at special discounts for sales promotion, corporate gifts, fund-raising, or educational purposes. Special editions can also be created to specifications. For details, contact the Special Sales Department, Skyhorse Publishing, 307 West 36th Street, 11th Floor, New York, NY 10018 or info@skyhorsepublishing.com.

Skyhorse® and Skyhorse Publishing® are registered trademarks of Skyhorse Publishing, Inc.®, a Delaware corporation.

Visit our website at www.skyhorsepublishing.com.

10 9 8 7 6 5 4 3 2 1

Library of Congress Cataloging-in-Publication Data is available on file.

Cover design by Mona Lin

Print ISBN: 978-1-5107-5889-6
Ebook ISBN: 978-1-5107-5625-0

Printed in the United States of America

Contents

Contents

Trespass

> I was surprised, as always, by how easy the
> act of leaving was, and how good it felt. The
> world was suddenly rich with possibilities.
> —*Jack Kerouac, On the Road*

Ihave never been good at standing still for long. I have always placed myself in life situations where I get to leave. My work in show business kept me moving. Later, two terms as president of the Cat Fanciers Association had me traveling to corners of the world I would otherwise have never seen. It seems if I stay still too long, things in life attach to my soul, the way a lamprey diminishes a trout. Luckily, I have never had much trouble slipping out the door.

When the weight of life, the heavy oppression in the yoke of everyday responsibility accumulates, I feel a stirring to go. Stirring is the wrong word; that suggests something subtle. In my consciousness, this weight builds to the anguish of a scream. I sometimes fancy I was born free. As I get older, I realize I was born freer than I am today.

In the accumulation of life that leads to frustration, you can, still, throw off the chains and free yourself. When I finally get to the point where I need to leave . . . I leave. Nothing like an organized trip. I have the basic plan: I grab piles of stuff; I am going to run away and go fishing. The fishing is the gravy. The important thing is to throw as much of the right stuff as possible in the back seat and trunk. It is almost as important to leave something important back home, too. It creates the inadvertent cause that incorporates itself into the trip—something to return to.

I have given a name to the pure escape impulse—"freestyling." The purpose of freestyling is to slip off the chains of oppression, forgo responsibility, get in touch with your inner vagabond, and catch nice trout. Sometimes the species can change. Catch some nice bass. Catch some nice pike. How about grayling? Sometimes grayling sound far enough away.

Freestyling takes you as far away from home as you need to be. One of the best things about the actual asphalt highway is that is has the uncanny power to knock the angst right out of you. I remember being in Louisville, Kentucky, when I found out my daughter was pregnant. My daughter, who was a senior in college. The one on whom I had spent lots of money to send to the Netherlands for a semester to study safe sex and HIV. Irony aside, I was willing to kill the perpetrator. During the course of the twelve-hour drive, the road dissipated much of my anger. When I reached home, still less than thrilled, I was beginning to get philosophical. In the end, I was able to chalk it up to the power of sex. Every millstone has its own weight and distance required to relieve that weight.

I had thrown what I felt was the right amount of stuff in the car. I then drove to the local liquor store. I purchased a bottle of vodka, a bottle of rum, a couple fifths of bourbon, and a full case of single-malt whisky. The whisky was not to ruin my liver; instead I would use it for trespass fees—I would barter for access to fishing. With freestyling, there is no real plan. You never make reservations at fancy lodges. That would defeat the purpose. The catharsis comes in the unplanned freedom, like a milkweed seed floating to where it needs to be but directionless until it gets there. Inevitably, that kind of drifting leads me to knocking on doors asking permission to fish. Sometimes I add a box of nice chocolate to the offer. Over the years, that has helped me to get on some nice water.

Trespassing has developed a negative connotation in recent years. I think it is due to all those "No Trespassing" signs tainting what otherwise would be beautiful landscapes. We trespass anytime we are not on property we actually own. When you are allowed passage to a place you don't own, you are trespassing in a positive way. Some places still use the term "trespass fee" or "trespass permission" in a way that is more positive. Being a somewhat conservative person in my views of land ownership, I believe that if you own land you can decide what to do with it. When it comes to riparian water rights, I tend to have liberal views. I believe you can own the land around the water but the things that God gave us belong to us all. Specifically, the water and the fly-eating vertebrates that live in the water. I remember being in a bar out West. It was one of those expensive trout towns where very wealthy people have purchased some very fine land with blue-ribbon water running through it. Overhearing a conversation on the bar stool next to me really got to me. The man was obviously an owner of the type of homestead I just described. He was bemoaning the fact that some folks were catching nice trout downstream from his spread on public water. He was certain that many of those fish move down from his place. He was telling his company that he was contemplating (illegally) placing a sort of underwater fence that would prohibit "his" trout from being caught downstream by "those people." I kept thinking *douche bag* over and over again. I made sure I accidentally spilled a drink on him before I called it a night.

As I began my freestyle trip, I noticed my car was heading west. I found that to be interesting. When I pull out of my driveway while freelancing, I seldom really know where I am going. Occasionally a friend invites me, which sometimes tells me where I will end up. This trip had none of that. I was just going. The early miles pound the angst out of you. You start to think about what you threw into the car. Then you start to think about what you didn't throw into the car. Eggs. I forgot eggs. One of the things I live for on these trips is streamside coffee. I like to percolate it in a small aluminum pot. Some people call it cowboy coffee. There is no filter. You let the grounds roil in the pot. The most important thing is to get fresh egg shell in the water. I also add the egg. It has a taste that has become important to the whole freestyle experience. So here I was, just east of Chicago, looking for eggs.

Somewhere between Chicago and Denver I stopped to buy eggs. I figured I was maybe a day away from needing them. I pulled into a convenience store. It wasn't a chain store; I dislike those. I root for the underdog. Aside from that, businesses that are run by individuals tend to take on some of the owner's personality. We used to call that flavor Americana. It is getting harder to find, but I still look for it. Big chains may save you ten cents for a candy bar but that has a cost. Walmart has no soul. Exposure to sterile, soulless environments chips away at your own individuality.

This place was just the opposite. There were photos of ten-dollar lottery winners taped to the front counter. They all had captions written under them requiring inside knowledge to get them. When I got to the egg refrigerator I noticed an end-of-row Coke display. This was a bit different. These were six packs of glass bottles. Across the red carton was printed *Hencho en Mexico*. Made in Mexico. It also meant something more. This Coke from Mexico was made with pure cane sugar. Strangely, I was excited about it. American Coke is made with corn syrup. Corn syrup is cheaper. Though many have tried suggesting that corn syrup tastes the same as pure cane sugar, it doesn't. It is the difference between a steamy shit sandwich and a perfectly cooked prime-rib sandwich. I walked away from the checkout counter with two dozen eggs and two dozen Mexican Cokes.

Several days after I purchased the eggs and Coke, I really didn't know what day of the week it was. That's how I know the freestyle is working. I could have grabbed my phone and found out, but I didn't want to know. I had fished that day. In fact, the evening blue-wing olive hatch was perfect. I had set up camp in one of those primitive campsites you can still find. For five dollars a night you have a spot you can set a tent on. It had a grill and a fire pit. Down the road was an immodest bath house with a toilet and a shower that ran, at best, cool. I had eaten dinner. I made pasta with a delicious red sauce that keeps well. I built a fire. You could buy bundles of well-dried hardwood at the camp "store." I was sitting in the dark facing my fire. Nobody knew I was there and nobody there knew who I was. That's as close to freedom as you can get anymore. I was enjoying that freedom. I had a glass—actually an enamel-covered tin mug—of bourbon with Coke made with cane sugar and lots of ice. I have learned to value ice. I have spent significant time in Europe and they seem to dislike ice. You never just get it in your glass, not even in a restaurant. You have to ask for it, and then, maybe no. It could be blazing heat, 100-plus degrees, and you still will not get ice. Thankfully, ice is readily available and cheap in America and it also holds up pretty well in any decent cooler. It kept my eggs cool, allowed me to keep cream for my cowboy coffee (not as necessary as eggs but damn pleasant) and, most important, let me have drinks on the rocks.

I was just relaxing in front of the fire. I had my shoes off and was sitting in the dirt. It was that real dry, dusty dirt, the kind that feels good between your toes. I was sipping the Coke-and-bourbon, looking at the stars, and thinking mostly about nothing. I enjoy that. Here and there organized thoughts would seep in. I was thinking about my ultimate freestyle. I have always wanted to take a trip with my Grand Laker canoe. A Grand Laker canoe is a model that was developed in Grand Lake Stream, Maine. They are made of wood strips covered with a fiberglass shell. Their length is usually between eighteen and twenty-two feet. They have a square transom to support a small motor, and also have a wide enough beam and big comfortable seats, which makes them very stable. They are great fishing boats. The other part that is so beautiful is that you tow them on a trailer, which, coupled with their light weight, makes them easy to launch almost anywhere. On my ultimate freestyle trip I trailer the canoe all across Canada, taking a whole summer and fishing from east to west. No plan, just getting on rural roads and stopping at any of the millions of lakes that call to me. I have been threatening to do this for a number of years now. I think most of my family and friends think it is just a pipe dream. I know it isn't. It is the dream of my soul.

I drifted away from thinking about that trip. Then I drift back, looking at the twinkling stars, thinking about the planets that are moving around them, wondering what kind of truck I would use for that trip across Canada. John Voelker has a chapter in his book, *Trout Madness,* called "The Fish Car." It is about outfitting a car in a way to make it ultimately utilitarian for fishing. I had mulled it over enough to decide that it needed to be a 1970s Ford model F-100. I would want it to be very clean and have those small round chrome hubcaps. It would have to have the original AM/FM radio. Part of the charm would be the chore of keeping a signal on the thing. It meant listening to the county farm report in Prairie Home, Nebraska. I would put a matched cap on the back. When it was standing before me, she would tell me what kind of modifications I needed to add to make her my fish car. I hope that it includes a mattress of some sort, special compartments for fishing and cooking gear, and perhaps even some sort of cool humidor. We'll see.

The next thought that permeated my head was cutthroat trout. I knew that the following day I would be near some places where I could fish for them. The thought of that brought a smile as I drew another gulp of sugar cane and corn mash. I love cutthroat trout. They have the same feel as my beloved brook trout. Like my brook trout, which is native to and belonged in the East, cutthroat are native and belong in the West. They both have received a bad rap. There was a time when some flyfisherman felt that both were dumb, too aggressive, and didn't provide the proper challenge. What could be better than a stunningly gorgeous fish that comes readily to a fly? Beyond that, they both have spent ages evolving to be an important part of their environments. For a reason I cannot name, it's important to me that the fish be as they were created. Thankfully those low IQ fishermen have been exposed as the dumbasses they are and both fish have been given their rightful and lofty place in our sport. Brook trout are the "home" guys and hold that special spot for me. If I lived in the West, they would easily get bumped by the cutthroat. My train of thought drifted to their further similarities, like the need for cool clean water, their stunning coloration, and how having one on the end of a bamboo rod is as close as I can get to heaven. Sometime during pleasant cutthroat memories, I drifted away into a deep restful sleep. I never even made it back to the tent.

The following morning had me driving along a nice stream that I knew held the fish I was looking for. It had that mixed look that is becoming too familiar along Western streams. There were million dollar homes, and then a few older spreads, then another fishing mansion, and then older homes. The invasion was well underway. I drove past a log cabin that seemed to be a good distance from the last big, new house. It had hummingbird feeders all around the front porch. It had a warm and inviting feeling. I decided that this would be the place I would first try to get permission to trespass. I walked up to the door on a walkway created with large local fieldstones that surfaced with the clearing of land. The stone had been there long enough that moss was well-established between the stones. The whole place had the feel of allowing life to find its niche.

I rapped firmly on the door. This was the part that always gives me anxiety. It makes me feel like a door-to-door Kirby salesman. The cold call is the most brutal sales technique ever. This was the hardest moment. The time from the knock until the door opens. It can and has run the gamut. I can vividly recall hauling ass back to the vehicle just ahead of dogs that were clearly enjoying it more than me. I can see a time very soon when my hauling is not enough and I become a chew toy.

I have learned that you must look as presentable as possible. If you look like you may have slipped off a passing train, you will have very little chance. As much as I hate to shave during a freestyle, a close shave is a must. I also have learned to leave the fishing rod and fly bag in the car. It conveys too much confidence. A fly vest, a clean shave, and a sincere smile has been my best approach. I could hear the footsteps. The door opened and an older man stood there.

"Hi," I said, "My name is Jerry and I was wondering if I could fly fish on your property?" At the same time, I thrust forward the chocolate and whisky. He looked me up and down. He had on a pair of denim overalls that were faded to almost white. His hair was totally white, and I tried to figure out his age. I was also under scrutiny and was trying to keep cool. "Do you have anything other than that high-end swill?" He snorted at me.

"I have some vodka and some rum," I offered.

"Doncha have any bourbon?" He snorted at me again.

I was at a point of crisis. I did have some but I had been hitting the bottle. I wondered if offering anything but a full bottle would look bad. "I have three-quarters of a bottle of Jack," I blurted out.

"Holding back the good stuff?" he replied in a low gravely tone. I tried to read this situation, but I couldn't. "You better go get it before it becomes two thirds of a bottle."

I briskly and happily walked back to the car. I grabbed my gear and the bottle of Jack. When I got back to the door, I noticed the chocolate and single malt were gone. "Here you go." I smiled as I thrust the bottle at him.

"Are you planning on keeping any fish?" he asked.

"If it wouldn't be too much to ask, I was hoping on one," I lied, really. I wasn't even thinking about it. He opened the door, so I took a swing for a trout dinner.

"No," he said. "One isn't going to do it. You're going to need to keep two cause the first one is mine."

"You know," he went on further, "I don't usually let hippies on the place!" He was pointing at the tie-dye shirt I had on under my fishing vest.

"Really, I am more a reformed hippy than anything." I tried to recover. *How could I have worn tie dye*, I thought, *shit!* I kept smiling.

"No matter," he said. "I will see you later. Don't forget my trout." He turned and walked back into the cabin. I did happen to notice a peace sign embroidered in fine beadwork on his back left pocket.

I began walking toward the stream. Just past the end of the driveway sitting a few yards into the field was an old pickup truck. As I got closer, I noticed it was about a 1971 Ford F-100. I recalled my deliberation the evening before and smiled at the irony. This truck had been there a while; she had sunk into the earth up to her axles. She was going to stay there. Past the truck was a field of golden prairie grass. The stream cut through the field like a blue ribbon on a gold dress. I walked toward the water with a building sense of excitement. This stream was a cutthroat stream. Though I knew there were stories of bull trout, they were akin to sightings of bigfoot or the Loch Ness monster. The day was calm with the occasional gust of wind. You could see the clouds move across the field over the stream and onto the neighboring property. When I was close enough to the water, I noticed that as the wind blew past the edge of the grass there would be multiple rises. "Terrestrials," I thought to myself with a real glee. Dry flies are the pinnacle of my fly fishing. The rare day when the fish are tuned into terrestrials is a special treat. I stopped and pulled out the fly book in which I had carefully placed rows of terrestrial flies. On the left side of the book were rows of Whitlock Hoppers lined up like soldiers in rank. These were real Whitlock Hoppers. My father had purchased bags of them more than two decades earlier. I recalled being at a fly-fishing show several months earlier. Dave was selling his hoppers in a signed shadow box for forty dollars apiece. I looked at the book and realized that I had a couple grand in Dave's Hoppers. I laughed to myself as I picked out one carefully to tie on. I have mixed feelings about fly-fishing collectables. To not use the best equipment in the sport seems wrong. It used to get to me. It does not bother me as much anymore. It's important to preserve history in almost any part of life. I get that. Fly fishing has such an artistic and storied history that it needs preserving. I have a book of flies that I had Lee Wulff sign. I guess I should put aside a few of Dave's Hoppers and have him sign them, too.

I watched the water carefully and picked a place to start fishing. I stayed back from the water a bit to avoid spooking anything. It is one of the things I love about Western fishing. You can really get flamboyant with your casting as there is really nothing around to get hung up on. Fly fishing in a wide-open area is a real treat, unlike at home in the East. I have decorated many trees and bushes with some pretty flies.

I could see the gust of wind coming for quite a distance. I would wait for it to roll down the hill pushing grass aside. When it came to the edge of the stream, I would time my cast so that my hopper would hit the water at the right time. The first cast was taken by a cutt with a zeal that was thrilling. I could feel the head shake telegraph all the way to the butt of my bamboo rod. Moments later I was holding in my hands an honest to goodness pure cutthroat trout. I stood there staring at the fish as I would a painting in a museum. There is something about cutthroat trout that get me. I was admiring the blood red gashes on her gill plates when she gave a shake as if to say, "I am glad to let you admire me but I am the one holding my breath."

I released the fish gently. I have caught only a few pure strain cutthroats in my life. Being from the East puts them far away. There are other reasons. Cutthroat trout have had a hard time of it. The usual problems of habitat quality and loss have adversely affected the fish. The biggest threat has come from their close cousins, the rainbow trout. Rainbow trout have been extensively stocked through much of the cutthroat range. They readily inter-breed, creating the villainous cutbow hybrid trout. Even that in recent times most places have stopped stocking rainbow trout, the damage has been done. In many waters you have fish that look like they might be some kind of cutthroat trout. Some folks claim that you can tell how much cutthroat they have in them by the length of the red slash on their gill plate. That is utter bullshit. If you have any genetic knowledge you know what is being expressed phenotypically is not necessarily what is going on with genotype. Only complex genetic testing can give you the results. Luckily there are a few drainages and lakes that didn't get fucked with and are the way they came off the universe's draft-ing board. This place was like that. It just felt right as rain and it soothed my soul.

Later that morning I came to a large deep pool. In a moment, a big head poked up out of the water to engulf a bug. I could see the nares from where I stood. If you can see the nostrils of a fish from fifteen yards away, you are in the presence of a big fish. The moment after the head poked up, I instinctively looked around. I always do that. It must be hard wired. I knew I was deliciously alone. That was altered a bit; I had a giant trout as company. Whenever that happens I get monster fever. That is a type of nervousness when confronted with a true trophy. I carefully tied on a new and bigger hopper. With shaking hands, I tested the knot. I waited for the wind to race across the meadow. Timing my cast, I set the fly upon the water. A moment later I had a firm take. It was not the giant. I gingerly fought the nice eighteen-inch trout downstream, all the while trying not to create too much disturbance in the pool. Moments later I was back in position. My eyes keenly watching for the next gust to blow across the golden prairie grass.

The wind eventually came and I set the fly up in the air in a way that the gust set it down almost perfectly. (I wonder why I cannot lay down a cast like that when other people are around.) The fly twitched for the briefest of moments. The take was subtle and stern. I set the hook and in that moment felt naked. I knew that the five-weight bamboo was in peril. In most cases you try to impart pressure on the fish via the rod. Using that pressure to tire and turn the fish during the fight. The light rod (relative to this fish) was going to make this fight interesting. The fish ran up to the head of the pool. The fish dug down at the far end of the pool. Deeper she went. The pool had a deep hole that shimmered blue green but made it impossible to see the bottom. I would pull back on the rod until it creaked and moaned, sounds a bamboo rod should never make. Then the leader snagged on something. With the line having no give, it was easy for the behemoth to give a powerful thrust of her tail and separate the fly from the line. My heart fell as the slack line drooped back toward me.

Some guys would say that they saw the fish and had it on for a while, that they were going to release it anyway, so it counts.

There are others that would shout "LDR," which stands for "Long Distance Release." The sentiment is the same as the first, claiming a sort of victory out of the situation. I do understand the value of the fight. The problem with those statements is that they disrespect the fish. It is like a topflight boxing match. The pool is the ring, the line is the medium, and the contest persists until there is a decision. Plain and simple, after an epic struggle, I lost. She (most trout of very large sizes are usually female.) won the contest. In fly fishing, losing is very important. If the outcome was assured, then where is the sport? I was lucky enough to have the fight. I knew two things, that this fish was not likely to take a fly again for at least a day or two, and this was the queen of the stream. (There is always a chance that another fish of that size lives near there, but very unlikely.) So that was it. I lost the big fight. At least there was the consolation prize. It is well accepted that the vanquished is allowed to play fast and loose with the truth as it pertains to the size of the victor. As it stands today, that cutthroat trout was a solid twelve pounds.

I fished the rest of the day in what would be the best cutthroat fishing I have ever had. I landed three fish that had reached the big fish standard of twenty inches. I had caught and released enough fish that I lost count. Really, those are the best days, when the fishing is so good that it stops needing to be quantified. It was a day that had the overtones of perfection. The landscape was the postcard beauty that was needed to house a world-class cutthroat fishery. The sun was bright and warming yet not hot. It had the rare quality that rocky mountain summer days treat us to during their short season. I started to notice the sun lowering into an early evening setting. In that backdrop, I could daydream my life away. Yet, there is always that realization that abruptly pulls the plug on the daydream . . . I forgot to keep fish. "Oh shit!" I remember thinking. I wasn't too concerned. I had fished the property hard but I was confident I could get at least one for my gracious host.

In a short while, I did manage to take two nice trout. They were fat and healthy. Both were in the seventeen-inch range on the small tape measure I carry in my vest. You could hold them in your hands and their girth would bulge between your fingers. I carefully prepared a fish stick. Not the kind in the freezer section—but the kind you create streamside with your favorite pocket knife. Rod in one hand, fish in the other, I walked back toward the house. It was a picture that was timeless. I could have been doing this very thing a hundred years ago and nothing would be different.

I walked to the front of the cabin where I found my host sitting on a double rocker with a woman by his side. "Looks like you had a good day," the man said as he eyed the two fat fish.

"Yes sir, I sure did," I smiled and replied.

"Sir? Don't call me sir. It makes me feel old." He smiled.

"To be honest," I said, "I didn't get your name."

He said, "That's because I didn't give it to you!"

The conversation was like waltzing with a porcupine. At that moment, the woman seated next to him threw him a sharp elbow to the ribs. It was a brisk reminder of the manners she expected.

He rose with a big smile and extended his paw, "Hi there, Jerry, my name is Jim and this pretty lady next to me is my wife Katy." As she stood to extend a hand in greeting it was easy to see she was pretty. She had long salt-and-pepper hair neatly braided and pulled forward over her left shoulder. Her green eyes danced with joy. It seemed to be her nature. Even the wrinkles on her face supported a genuine smile. She wore a cotton blouse that was covered with embroidery and beadwork that attested to great skill. Her skirt was a simple Indian print and it all came together in a sophisticated bohemian fashion statement. To look at them together you just had to assume they were soul mates. "Let Jim take those fish," she said. "Why don't you come on in?"

I was taken aback a bit. I was feeling a bit shy and was trying to find the words that would excuse me while at the same time express my gratitude. It felt like Jim was looking right through me.

"I must tell you that you are staying for dinner!" Jim stated with a little authority. "Katy has set three place settings at the dinner table. We just won't take any other answer besides yes."

I shook my head yes. I was really liking these people. They had a warm gentleness to them. I was shown to the parlor. Jim told me to make myself at home. He was going to dress the trout and he would be "back in a "jiffy." I sat in the overstuffed chair I was led to. It was the kind that was popular in the fifties. It was stuffed with goose down, large with a high back and big arm rests. The fabric was a solid mauve sculpted floral pattern. I sat in the chair and sank into it in a way that caused me to emit an involuntary "*ahh*." After a full day of wading, the chair hit the spot. I noticed a few feet away was a matching couch. In front of the couch was an old faded cherry coffee table. On top of the table was a multicolored doily that looked like the kind of thing made in front of a fire during cold Rocky Mountain winter nights. Upon the beautiful lace doily was a book. Being a bibliophile, I recognized it almost instantly. It was a first edition of Jack Kerouac's *On the Road*. Though my bones were really digging the comfort of the chair, my brain was ordering all my body parts to commence the rise sequence. I carefully lifted the book and opened the cover. Much to my surprise, there was an inscription. As I read it, pins and needles permeated my body. "To Jim and Katy, See you next summer, Jack." In that moment the book went from collectable to relic. I didn't even have the chance to feel guilty when Jim walked in. "I am so sorry," I said. "I collect books and recognized it. I just wanted to see it."

Jim cut me off. "Hey man, no worries. We keep it there so people *can* see it."

"You knew Jack Kerouac?" I asked in a tone of awe.

"Katy and I ran around in some of the same circles. You know, coffee houses and poetry readings. Katy was a pretty special beat poet. That's how I fell in love with her. You know, same old story, beautiful poet falls in love with scruffy bongo player."

Jim went on to tell about how he met Katy and their early days, and what the "beat culture" was like. You could tell he was excited to have company. Jim ran out of the room and returned with the bottle I presented to him earlier. "How do you want your drink?" he said.

I looked at him, and then I looked at the bottle. "If I could," I said, "I would like a tall glass full of ice." I held up two fingers. "I would like that much Jack and then the rest filled with Coke."

Jim looked at me. "Aw man," he said, "we don't keep soda in the house very often. How about some fresh iced tea?"

"I have some Coke in the car," I said and smiled.

"Sure," he replied, "go get it."

I ran out to the car. I grabbed the six pack—only I noticed it had five Cokes. I had a pang of guilt. I felt like I was not being the complete guest. "What the hell," I thought. I had given him a bottle that was three-quarters full, how bad could it be bringing in a six pack that was five-sixths full?

When I returned with the soda, Jim's face lit up. Then Jim started shouting in an excited tone. "Katy! Katy come here!" I began looking around trying to figure out what the excitement was. As Katy entered the room, Jim snatched the sodas from my hand. He still had the excited tone. "Look here. *Hecho* Coke!" He showed her with delight.

Katy looked at the Mexican Coke and replied to Jim's excited state. "Aw jeez, he's one of you!" She sported a big grin as Jim explained how they were usually opposed to soft drinks, but there was one exception: Mexican Coke. He went on further to explain that it could not be found in the nearby town and that on their infrequent trips to the big city, they always returned with a case. The only fitting mixer for Jack was Mexican Coke, and he was truly delighted. Moments later, and with Jim's care of a professional mixologist, we all were sporting tall glasses of his preferred concoction. It's funny how little things can matter. Any awkwardness of being a stranger was gone. The evening had taken on a celebratory tone.

Not long after, Katy summoned us to the dinner table. It was set in simple exquisiteness, with an arrangement of wild flowers in the center. At each place was a salad with a simple yet delicious garlic-and-lemon dressing. Katy informed me that the salad and garlic came from their garden. On a large serving platter was the cutthroat trout prepared in a beautiful amandine next to a bowl of small potatoes seared in rosemary. The entire meal came off the property. I realized I wasn't wrong to wear the tie-dyed shirt that day: instead of being an impediment, it probably helped me.

Dinner was as tasty as it looked. The conversation was pleasant, with the right amount of polite pauses that a truly delicious dinner demands. The dessert was a homemade blueberry pie, still warm from the oven. Katy was a culinary genius.

With full bellies, we retired to the porch with fresh drinks. Jim and Katy told story after story. There were tales about Jack Kerouac and Neal Cassidy. Jim talked about playing a coffee house in Connecticut with the Lamp Lighters. How he once sat in with the Kingston Trio. There was music playing softly behind us. It was a live recording of an acoustic Hot Tuna concert. It filled the pauses in the conversation nicely, and I even got lost in it during an exceptionally good rendition of "Hesitation Blues." Politely I drifted back to the conversation. Drinks flowed and the gods treated us to a breathtaking Rocky Mountain sunset. More wonderful than all of that was the friendship created. One that would last all our days.

As will happen, time moved along and glasses became empty and the evening drew to a close. At their insistence, I would stay in the spare bedroom. "You must stay, Jerry," Katy spoke in subdued tones. "You have drunk and should not drive."

"I agree," I said softly, too. "I am so glad I stopped here today."

Jim chimed in, "It is so infrequent that we have guests anymore. It was a true pleasure."

Katy added, "That spare room has been unused for at least a year. I forget how nice company can be."

Jim patted me on the back. He then took me to the spare room. It was simply yet warmly decorated. The queen bed had nice Egyptian cotton linen. I opened the window a crack. A breeze of cool mountain air snuck in under the sash. I settled into the bed, as comfortable as it looked. The night noises came into the room with the breeze. I thought about the day. I thought about the big fish. I thought about catching honest to goodness pure-strain cutthroat trout. I thought about my new friend. How if we let life run its course the treasures we get are endless. I would have thought about a whole lot more except sleep found me fast and I was fast asleep.

Morning came without fanfare. When you wake up in a strange place, you rewind the memory tape to orient yourself. I looked up at the white ceiling and started to think again. Something smelled good; breakfast was cooking. Eggs and some kind of breakfast meat. Ham or maybe sausage, I wasn't sure. I felt good. My soul felt good. I was whole again. It was time to go home. I cleaned up in accordance with my morning ritual. In a short time, I was ready to leave the room. I looked around one last time. It's a habit to make sure nothing is forgotten. I also do it to add a visual snapshot for my life memory.

Breakfast sausage. Also eggs and pancakes. Katy truly was an amazing cook. Even though I had just met them, saying goodbye was not easy. It was a testament to what nice folks they are. I promised I would be back. I meant it. I loaded what "stuff" I had into the car. I made a mental note to send a case of *Hecho* Coke.

As I sat in the driver's seat, I noticed I was opposite that old Ford truck. It made me smile a melancholy smile. The bones of the truck stood out against the morning sun. In that moment I decided that the quest for my fish car would need to start with finding a 1971 Ford F-100. For an old truck at the end of its road, that old Ford had a lot to say.

As I looked at the truck some more, I realized that it took my new friends to the place where they ended their road days. It felt bittersweet. They were off the road but they landed in a place off the grid. (Symbolically at least—they had running water and electricity.) They had found a special place and they were free. They managed to be souls that slipped from Big Brother's radar. They were quiet and innocuous and Big Brother never missed them. Hopefully, I can go slip sliding off the radar, too.

Double-Hauling along
the Milky Way

Two possibilities exist: Either we are alone
in the Universe or we are not. Both are
equally terrifying.

—*Arthur C. Clarke*

In the world of fly fishing, the brook trout has a certain mystique.
The fish doesn't attain a particularly large size, and it doesn't fight
especially hard, but it is stunningly beautiful. Its hold on us can be
seen from the sheer volumes of literature written about the pretty
little fish. Nick Karas's book, simply titled *Brook Trout*, to John
Gierach's *Even Brook Trout Get the Blues*, and all the brook-trout
books in between demonstrate the lofty prominence of brook
trout in our sport. I understand the pull of these pretty little fish.
Every year I do my best to be in northern Maine during the last
week of June so I can fly fish for brook trout during the amazing
Green Drake mayfly hatch at about that time.

As often as not, regardless of how hard I try, ignoring all the
record keeping I use, nature thumbs her nose at my best attempts
to prognosticate, and I miss the temperamental Green Drake

hatch. Most of the time, the week I choose does have at least a day or two on a certain lake where the magic happens, and I catch lots of beautiful northern Maine brookies on big Green Drake dry flies. It feels pure and righteous. It offers proof that fly fishing can be, at its best, high art. This past year was different. The spring was wonky and all over the board. I whiffed. The previous year was perfect, but this past year was humbling. After a few days of chasing the dragon, I could tell it was time to raise the white flag. There is always next year.

In rethinking my strategy, last spring I decided to do a few things I had always wanted to do but never got around to. There is a lake in Maine's Allagash Wilderness Waterway that has captured my attention. When we talk about wilderness we usually talk about places with a certain anonymity. Places that are old and wild and whose names have disappeared on the wind long ago. There are places in the wilderness where notable events earned them a well-known name. Eagle Lake in the Allagash Wilderness is such as place and has such acclaim.

I hired a local guide to take me there. There were certain spots I wanted to see and local knowledge was needed to find the precise places. We would meet at the museum near the Churchill Dam. Last summer marked the fiftieth anniversary of the creation of Allagash Wilderness Way. This made getting to the museum a bit early worth the effort just to see the special displays that were there to commemorate the milestone. When I was there, I ran into a biologist and we discussed Eagle Lake. He felt the next state brook trout record would come out of the lake. There had often been whispers about big brookies, but hearing it from a biologist made it concrete.

The guides I hired showed up on time. They trailed a large, wide, and stable Scott canoe. I loaded up my fly-fishing gear and a map of the area. We would head south from the dam and go through Heron Lake, into Churchill Lake, into Round Pond, into

Little Eagle Lake, and finally onto Eagle Lake. When we arrived at Eagle the weather was rainy and windy. My guides decided to troll to our destination at the south end of the lake. Actually, there were two destinations. The first was Pillsbury Island. My interest there was to see the farthest north Henry David Thoreau ever stayed. There are two campsites on Pillsbury Island. The one on the west side of the island is called Thoreau and the one on the east side is called Pillsbury Island Campsite. Thoreau stayed at the east site, not the west. Oops. Pillsbury was the furthest north Thoreau ever went. He described and named all the flora and fauna in and around his site.

"I give these names because it was my farthest point north," he wrote. Thoreau's *Maine Woods* was three essays. The poetry in those essays makes me believe Thoreau was a flyfisherman, although there is no proof. He did refer to the Eastern brook trout in his Maine writings as "Bright Fluviatile Flowers," and "In the night I dreamed of trout-fishing; and, when at length I awoke, it seemed a fable that this painted fish swam so close to my couch . . . "

One of the things I was looking forward to was taking a shore lunch near the couch Thoreau described. My guides promised me an epic North Woods shore lunch. Before we would dine in the steps of Thoreau, I wanted to see another spot that was coincidentally within sight of where Thoreau stayed. Weeks earlier I was looking around on the internet to see what was going on in conjunction with the fiftieth anniversary celebration of the creation of the Allagash Wilderness Waterway. While doing this I stumbled on results for something called the "Allagash Abductions." Many thousands of results showed up in my internet search. In a strange case of parallelism, this event was observing its fortieth anniversary. The Allagash Abductions allegedly took place in August 1976. Four young college students went to find Mother Nature in the recently-formed Allagash Wilderness Waterway. The story, very basically and briefly, goes something like this: Four young men, twin brothers Jim and Jack Weiner and friends Chuck Foltz and Charles Rak, stayed at a campsite on Eagle lake. They decided to go night fishing. They saw a strange light in the sky. One of them shined a flashlight at it. The craft came closer and shined a blue beam into the water. Years later, they would undergo hypnosis and regress to the event. During the regression, they described a bizarre event of being abducted and experimented on by extraterrestrial life forms.

Somewhere in the article, it stated that three of the four were giving lectures for various UFO research groups. It seems the fourth man, Charles Rak, "Has been out of contact with the group for more than two decades and could not be located . . ." I wondered about that so I tried to find Chuck. After a ten-minute search, I was on the phone with him. Sometimes people don't want to look very hard. In this case I found out why. Chuck's story was very different. Actually, it was the same up till the abduction. He was a very nice man and stated that the story was true to the point where the craft shined the blue beam. After hovering above Eagle Lake for a length of time with the blue beam shining into the water, Charles said that "it shot up very quickly and then disappeared from sight." No abductions, just a strange occurrence.

I am not sure why the whole story stuck with me. I would read articles and watch videos. There were volumes about the case. In the end, I knew I had to see the place. I am really not sure why. Maybe to see if I could get a "feel" for the place that might help me make up my mind on the story.

My guides knew the exact spot. As the boat neared the camp site, a large man hurried to where his canoe was beached and looked at us with arms crossed.

"Hey there," I greeted the tall man.

"What can I do for you?" he snapped back.

"I just wanted to see the camp where the 'Allagash Abductions' had supposedly taken place."

"It's all a bunch a shit!" the man said. "I was here that night and no one was taken anywhere."

"You were here?" I asked with a big smile. "What did you see?"

It was then that weird got weirder. The man started to become irate. His voice raised. "Not a goddamned thing. Them boys is just a bunch of drug-taking liars. I stay here almost all the time I can. If they come back, they need to talk to me!" As he was barking at us he walked into the water as if he was going to push our canoe. It was then that my guide spoke up.

"Hey friend," he said. "I wouldn't put a finger on my canoe. We're just doing a little sightseeing; we're going to be moving along."

"I see," said the man, calming a bit. "How's the fishing today?"

"Been a little slow," my guide said. "We caught two or three fall fish for every trout we got." After a brief pause my guide asked, "I didn't catch your name."

"Charbonneau," he said. "Everybody calls me Charbonneau. I am always here if you need me. You best move on now. I got some wood to chop. Yep, a big pile of wood."

He started to get nervous and fidgety. We said our goodbyes and headed off to Pillsbury Island. The Pillsbury Island site was pretty and well-maintained. I sat at the table, in the aura of Henry David Thoreau's shadow, as my guides started to fix their legendary North Woods feast. In a few short moments after we started setting up for lunch, a big hare showed herself. It seems the local wildlife has gotten used to visitors and waits for them. I raided the cooler and took a few strands of lettuce and some carrots from the salad container. As I watched the hare eating the offerings, I couldn't help but notice the parallels between the hare and Charbonneau. I began to think about all the events that seemed to intersect at this wilderness spot. Seeing the spot where the alleged abductions took place gave me a weird vibe. Why would E. T. come here? Maybe it was about Thoreau and brook trout—that's why I came. Maybe there was a planet three or four light years farther out on the left arm of the Milky Way spiral. Maybe that planet is primarily a watery world that is cooler than Earth. Maybe it has two bright golden moons, lots of streams, rivers, lakes, and oceans. Maybe the primary life is all kinds of aquatic insects like purple drakes, paisley duns, and electric-blue salmon flies. Maybe the water also holds various kinds of minnow-type fish. Maybe E. T. became enamored with brook trout and wanted to make that watery world complete. It would explain the blue beam shining into Eagle Lake. I sure hope they remembered to take some bamboo with them, too!

Kodachrome

I got a Nikon camera
I love to take a photograph
So mama don't take
my Kodachrome away.

—*Paul Simon*

They say a picture is worth a thousand words. I guess that depends. In Rochester, New York, where I am from, a picture meant more than that. Kodak was the company that defined Rochester. If your family didn't work at Kodak directly, most likely a member of your family worked for a business that worked for Kodak. Kodachrome was a kind of color imaging that put Kodak in control of 90 percent of film sales and 85 percent of camera sales in the US as late as 1976. In 1975, an electrical engineer and Kodak employee named Steven Sasson invented digital photography. A few years later, Kodak decided to ditch its interest in digital photography because they controlled the silver-nitrate market. There is an infamous memo out there from company leadership shunning digital photography, thereby eventually killing the company and destroying the fabric of a whole city. So when someone asks what a picture is worth, the correct answer is, "it depends."

In fishing circles, photography has put limitations on that for which fishermen are best known—prevarication. It is hard to lie about the size of a fish when there is a photo. On the other hand, we get to keep the "Kodak Moment" forever. The other thing about the argument of a photo's worth versus the written word is that the argument depends on the words. What if the words tell a good story? Is the photo still worth a thousand words? What if it is a fishing story about a photo?

Dave is a Maine guide. He has been one for more than four decades. He was also a high-school science teacher. The biggest drawback to taking one of Dave's classes was that you might learn about hunting and fishing as well as the science of Kingdom, Phylum, Class, Order, Family, Genus, and Species. Dave has also accompanied my father when fly fishing for bass. They have shared a boat every June for decades. Their days are filled with fly fishing for bass and arguing about baseball. My father is a Yankees fan and Dave has his Red Sox.

After Dave has finished guiding my father, he guides another long-term client. Here, I'll refer to him as The Boy to protect his identity. When he first showed up almost forty years ago, The Boy was just that—a young boy. However, The Boy is now a man. He was born with a brain disability. It does not affect the fact that he is a thoughtful, sensitive, caring human being. Over the years, Dave and The Boy have established a special relationship. The Boy's father, in seeking ways to share life with his son, came to Grand Lake Stream in Maine to fish. Like so many others, such as Ted Williams and Lee Wulff, the man and his son fell in love with Grand Lake Stream and the area's wonderful bass fishing. Over time, they would spend a little time at Fenway Park watching the Red Sox play baseball and then head up to Maine. Recently, the father and son were going to the ballgame before the fishing trip. With the heighted security of our time, The Boy's pocket knife was found at the ballpark. The security agent asked The Boy what the knife was for? The Boy, a little despondent, told security, "It's important that I get my knife back! I need it to cut the potatoes for shore lunch." The father explained the situation to security. It illuminates how the ritual of fishing was profound in The Boy as it is in many of us. The fishing is important. The harvesting of a couple bass or white perch for shore lunch is important. The peeling and cutting of the potatoes is important. Photographing each and every fish is important.

It seems that when The Boy was in his early teens, his father purchased a 35mm camera for him to take on fishing trips. From that trip on, The Boy has used that camera to snap images of every fish he has ever caught. The ritual was a vertical shot. Or a horizontal shot. Or sometimes a photo of the fish and The Boy. Sometimes a shot of the fish and Dave. For more than thirty years, many hundreds of bass have been in the aperture of that Nikon camera.

Last season, The Boy came up to Grand Lake Stream, as he had done for thirty-something seasons before. The father, now older and frailer, knowing how important this trip is to his son, made the trip as well. Nowadays, the father finds other things to do while Dave and his son fish. On a fine summer day, the two went fishing like they always have. They harvested a couple of smaller bass and broke bread in the tradition of the shore lunch. That morning, like every other morning the two had fished, The Boy carefully loaded his prize camera into the boat. He carefully took it out of its protective case, cleaned the lenses, and made sure it was in shape for the day's action. Then every fish, even the ones bound for the frying pan, were photographed at least three times.

That afternoon after shore lunch, The Boy hooked the biggest bass in his thirty-year fishing career. The fish jumped. The fish tail walked. The fish tried going under the boat and around the motor. It seems that after all those years of fishing under Dave's skillful hand, The Boy was an angler. An angler is something most fisherman aspire to (myself included). After the epic fight, the fish finally was netted. The Boy, realizing the poignancy of the moment, snapped more photos than usual. He instructed Dave to pose the fish this way and that. Very few supermodels have had such a rigorous photo shoot. In the fish's best interest, the shoot ended and the fish was released. They fished the rest of the day and caught and photographed a few more fish.

Dave eased the boat to the dock. Waiting there, as he does every time, was The Boy's father. He inquired about the fishing, as he always does. The Boy jumped on the dock and began an excited recounting of his biggest bass ever.

"Is that right?" the father asked in a tone of love and pride.

"Om, my goodness," Dave replied in his Maine accent. "It was all of five pounds."

"Oh, that is so wonderful," the father gushed.

Dave leaned in toward the father. "It was really a big one!" And then he said, "I like to keep photos of my clients with really nice fish. I would appreciate it if I could get a couple of copies of the photos."

"Photos?" The father queried.

"Yeah, copies of the pictures we took with his camera."

The father looked at Dave and a smile grew over his face. "There's no film in that camera."

"Not ever?" Dave asked.

"Not ever," the father stated with the broad smile still stretching.

The next day, Dave went to pick up The Boy at the dock. They went fishing. They had a shore lunch. The Boy cut the potatoes. They caught fish. Dave held the fish for the photos. Each and every one of them. Dave dropped The Boy off at the dock. The father was there to meet them and hear about the day. The same thing happened every day until The Boy's trip was done. As soon as it was, he (The Boy) started looking forward to coming back.

One of the greatest things about fishing is the way it can remove barriers among people. You can take people from anywhere and put them together and they might kill each other. You can take people from anywhere and put them together with fly rods in their hands and they will develop a loving friendship that will stand the test of time. I like this story because it is funny. I also like that it exposed the quirky nature of the sport, but most of all I like the way it gets us all in the same boat.

The question at hand is this: Is a picture worth a thousand words? The best answer is it depends. In this case, you would need the photo and a thousand words. It's like the line in the song "Kodachrome" by Paul Simon: "Mama don't take my Kodachrome away!"

Forbidden Love

Thank you, dear God, for this good life
and forgive us if we do not love it enough.
Thank you for the rain. And for the chance
to wake up in three hours and go fishing:
I thank you for that now, because I won't
feel so thankful then.

—*Garrison Keillor*

There are many rooms in the house of fishing. In breadth, it is large and varied. Oddly enough, at both ends of that house you'll find bamboo rods. On the one end, you have the simple cane rod with no reel. This is how many of us began to fish, with a long piece of mono attached to the tip, often with a bobber and a hook near the terminal end. This live-bait rig works well and, as I see it, has many similarities to the Japanese fishing method of *tenkara,* which uses no reel on the rod. Symbolically, an old flyfisherman grabs a *tenkara* rod to complete the circle around which fishing has led him.

The other end of the fishing spectrum is occupied by that same material, bamboo. This side of the house is usually occupied by longtime fishers. They have elevated their sport so that it approaches art. Some of these people have created a rigid realm and it is often perceived as pure and good.

Those men—usually they are men—are called purists. It is easy to become a casualty to the art, to become a true and egotistical asshole. I have to watch myself carefully. It would be easy to succumb to the temptation of becoming a purist. You have to keep reminding yourself that it is all a corporate smokescreen to get into your pants. That in the right hands, a $29.99 fly-fishing setup will work anywhere in the world.

I know most of you are thinking I am talking only about fly-fishing but every room has its tools. The commonality is ego—that is what has the anglers bent over a cash register while they are fleeced. Take the bass guys. The gaudy expensive rigs to chase largemouth bass are very pricey. The dream is the tournament trail. Ask one of them if they might be willing to take you in their boat to sneak up on carp with a "berry fly," and you will soon understand that the term "bass hole" describes more than just a good fishing spot.

All of that aside, I will stick to my rooms in the house of fishing. The ones where the line propels the lure and not the other way around. There are many in these rooms who feel that fly-fishing is the proper method of chase for the proper fish. They tend to call themselves purists. There are many shades of purists. The purest of the pure are probably all but extinct. They felt that the only worthy adversary was the Atlantic salmon. The air up there is pretty thin, particularly with the decline of wild fish stocks.

I have not encountered one of these guys in a while. I suspect many of them slid down the hill a tad and will only fish for trout (char being lumped in, too). They will occasionally slum it with Arctic grayling. Some folks have a larger base of core species than others. Then there are those who have absolutely no standards. They will fish for carp, drum, gar, or any other lowly nongame fish. They are the ones whispered about in the fly-fishing fraternity. You will never see them on the cover of an Orvis catalog holding up a big grass carp while wearing the newest spiffy duds.

It may be hard to believe, but there is a level even below this: Those who really don't give a shit about anyone else's standard. It is where I must confess being a proud member of the bottom dwellers.

Recently, I went fly fishing in Florida to escape the oppression of a very tough winter. (In my neck of the woods we broke the record for winter's coldest month. The coldest month of any month *ever*, for as long as they had been keeping track.) I know some of you are thinking, "Okay, cool, he was fishing for bonefish in the Keys." It gets worse than that.

I was freshwater fishing and not for largemouth bass. The truth is that I had come to fish for peacock bass in the urban canals in and around Miami. I had come across a guide who had some experience with flyfishermen and said that this was a good time to get 'em ("them" being peacock bass). While chasing peacock bass with a fly rod is okay on an exotic trip to the Amazon, it is far less so if they are invasive and urban. If you doubt this, try finding a peacock-bass-fly-fishing guide in the Miami area. Which is precisely what I did.

Almost all the guides who go after peacocks in South Florida are bait dunkers. They are shiner oriented. More than once I got, "Just to be clear, you don't wanna fish shiners?"

Eventually I found a gentleman named Rick Barnhart who said about 30 percent of his customers used fly tackle. When I told Rick that I wanted to book four straight days of peacock-bass fishing with a fly rod, the pregnant pause said it all. After the pause, I told him my goal was to catch a nice peacock with a bamboo rod. This led to pregnant pause number two. After confirming the dates—and several reaffirming phone calls later—you could tell Rick was getting into it. He wanted my trip to be successful, as he understood that opening the door to fly guys meant an expanded client base. Isn't that what all good businesses and businesspeople do?

Included in the questions I asked via phone was what kind of boat we would fish from? I was uncertain, as I understood that the canals were narrow, some less than twenty feet. (Most a bit wider, actually.) Rick told me I would be fishing off the back end of his bass boat, and that it had a nice big platform from which to cast. Images of giant rigs and obscene horsepower overtook my mind's eye. What could be further from the pastoral imagery flyfishermen envision for themselves? Take yours truly, a semi-reformed beat-nik—this could present some philosophical challenges.

As I worried if this was going to work, I also was telling myself that Rick was cool and the experience was going to be great. That first morning, I was to meet Rick at a local restaurant at 8:45. I was wondering about the late start (in fishing terms) but I was cool with it. I pulled into the Flannigan's parking lot, hold-ing my breath all the while. I pulled up to Rick and the rig, and I was pleasantly surprised on both counts. Rick was in his fifties, unshaven, and tan. He looked like what a *Miami Vice* actor might look like twenty-five years later. As the fishing days went on, my appraisal changed to *Miami Vice* meets the Grateful Dead 2015. A bit odd, but it worked. In fact it worked well.

The rig was the best possible outcome for me. She was about twenty years old with a faded black metallic paint job. She was smallish but the perfect size for two guys fly-fishing a canal. She had a utilitarian look and feel. I was so thankful that it did not take on cartoon proportions. I transferred all my stuff to Rick's truck. I noticed the absence of all the traditional fly-guide stuff—no leader material, no tippet, clippers, flotant, or line dressing. I wondered about his ability to guide a flyfisherman, and asked him if he could tie a nail knot. "Nope," he said. How about a blood knot? Again—"Nope." I tried again: Perfection loop? "Nope."

Double Surgeon's loop? It turned out he could tie a double clinch knot. To be fair, the double clinch knot is a great knot and, apart from some of the special needs of fly fishing, all that you really need. I did know that he was the only guy I could find who had some experience with flyfishermen. But Rick made it clear that most of his clients were bait-and-tackle guys.

As we were driving to the first day's fishing, Rick told me we were going to an area called the Blue Lagoon. Blue Lagoon? Here I was escaping the coldest month in history in Rochester, New York, and images of a tropical paradise flashed in my head. That was driven by memories of the pubescent fantasy film of the same name. The setting of the film was beautiful. The film itself sucked.

Names are funny. We often draw conclusions about something merely by its name. Comedian Stephen Wright helped us by noticing that we drive on parkways and park on driveways, jellyfish are neither jelly nor a fish, guinea pigs are not swine, and of course military intelligence is an oxymoron. The Blue Lagoon Lake in question is situated at the end of the cargo runway of the Miami airport. It's a misnomer by smelling of jet fuel, being noisy due to jets taking off and car noise from the highway right along its shore, and the fact that it is surrounded by large buildings. This hardly had the feel of a brief fly-fishing vacation to escape oppressive winter weather back home.

While it may not have been a tropical paradise, in time I would see its value. As we carefully worked along some cattails, Rick quickly pointed out a bed. I strained to see it. I was looking in the same spot as Rick but just couldn't see it. I left my good polarized sunglasses at home but had on the "cool" ones I had purchased at Walt Disney World days before. Before the fishing, I had taken my family to Disney as a treat for them, as well. There, a man sporting a Goofy hat at one of the Disney shops assured me these were "superior" polarized sunglasses. Telling you that you should be wary of salesmen wearing Goofy hats seems unnecessary now.

Eventually I started to cast according to Rick's directions. Within a half hour of leaving the dock, I had hooked my first peacock bass. It was a three-pound-plus beauty that ate a black Wooly Bugger fished on my 6-weight bamboo rod. The rod was a stout two-piece based on a Dickerson design. I was worried about the rod right after hook set. Peacock bass pull hard—really, it did surprise me. After a careful but enjoyable fight, Rick netted the fish. I could not wait to get my hands on it. Carefully I looked into it mouth and found the jaws to be very similar to largemouth bass. It had the same sandpaper texture that allowed it to be lipped.

The fish are just stunning. The variety in Florida is the butterfly peacock bass. The fish start out with dark green at the top, which then goes to a lighter green, fading to yellows and gold toward the belly. It has three dark bands (though not always) on its sides. Its tail has a false eyespot of black with a gold and yellow corona around it. During spawning, the bottom of the fish light up. The pectoral and pelvic fins turn bright orange, as does the throat and the bottom of the tail. It is a very handsome fish. Did I mention that a peacock pulls hard? I had accomplished my first goal, which was to catch a peacock bass on a bamboo fly rod.

We started at Blue Lagoon Lake that first day. Soon, it was obvious that the lake needed a bit more time for the fish to set up their spawning beds. Rick knew the canals would be further along. The canal system would take us into urban Miami. Though the temperature was warm, it was far from a tropical paradise. The canals were crossed often by many bridges and pipelines. They ran behind yard after yard; at times, it was hard for me to witness the urban pollution. This was not only *trash* pollution, but also *social* pollution. We would see homeless people living under bridges. There was evidence of cult activities, including Santeria. It was the seamy underbelly of the city. You could tell that, at one time, it was future planning at its best. In fact, it was the hundredth birthday of Miami Beach. Along the way many of the yards had boat launches and water patios. It was evident that many years had passed since they were last used. Miami had passed from a place of Jewish heritage to a senior citizen haven, and now it was steeped in a Latino culture. Many of the yards had bathtubs half buried with the Virgin Mary residing in the shelter. Being Italian, I was familiar with bathtub Mary or, as we affectionately called her, "Mary on the Half Shell." It was an indication of a Catholic community. I began to think of her as Mary of the Peacock Bass.

It was a sight to see all the once-affluent homes. Though they had declined as time marched on, you could see the old landscaping overgrown and gone wild. Many of the trees were in bloom. Bright reds and oranges and yellows and purples and blues and lush greens. It was pretty cover—almost alien in its isolation.

Stretches of the canals were overgrown in a way that made the waterway disconnected from the property to which it was adjacent. I felt like we were hiding in plain sight.

One canal would lead to an intersection with another canal. Some of these opened up into a pond-like situation. As we approached one of the intersections, a loud Latin brass sound screamed in the air. In a short while, the area from where the noise emanated came into view. It was a restaurant perched on the edge of the canal. The water amplified a guttural alfresco sound. The tables and furnishings were beat up and dirty. The smell of food was inviting, but it looked dangerous in both a physical and culinary way. I wanted to stay away, but then again a part of me wanted to go there, like the allure of a trashy woman wearing too much makeup.

"Hey Rick, is that place any good?" I asked.

He said he heard the food was very good. Then, after a pause he said: "I have never eaten there."

"You want to give it a try? I'll buy!" I said.

Rick maneuvered the boat to the bank. It was obvious that we were the first boat to park there in a long time. Every eye in the place was on us. The *gringos* had come by sea! The stares were fixed on us almost in disbelief. These moments can go very wrong or be very right. It usually depends on how the ice is broken. The gods were smiling on us, as in that moment a beautiful dark-eyed girl came to the boat and grabbed the rope. Following her lead, several men came and helped us tie off the boat. A dirty but delicious culinary delight followed. The things they did with pork cannot be described. Like any good fishing spot I will not tell where it is. The worst thing that could happen would be a bunch of white people starting to show up there.

The rest of the afternoon was warm and pleasant. It was for the most part a learning experience. It was the kind of day on which you just try to get a feel for the nuances of fly-fishing for peacock bass. We went down canal after canal. In the end, we fished miles of water. I had hooked and landed almost a dozen peacock bass and a couple of largemouth bass, as well. It was good to have the comparison to understand that there was no comparison. The peacocks pulled so fucking hard. The largemouth felt like a wet rag alongside the pretty fish. I asked myself if their beauty belied their attitude. In the thought process, I decided that they looked just right, almost as if they were on fire. They were colored in a way that I imagined dragons would be colored. That evening I sat in contemplation for a bit. I really couldn't grasp the fish just yet; I would need more time with them. The unfortunate part was I had agreed to fish the Everglades the next day primarily for largemouth bass.

Fishing the Everglades was something I was a bit hesitant about. Nothing is wrong with the area—in fact, the Everglades are a beautiful and amazing ecosystem. It is also an area that has been in real trouble.

Once man learned to drain a swamp and turn it into "useful" land he has seemed to want to do nothing else. It took years for smart people to figure out that these are vibrant and diversified ecosystems. Also, the Everglades are extremely important to all the ecosystems of the peninsula. After more than two centuries, the assault on the Everglades has turned around and, like most ecosystems, once given a break, will come back with vigor.

All that aside, the reason I didn't want to fish the Everglades was that I didn't want to fish for largemouth bass. Nature seemed to express my mood and provided a day with sustained winds of twenty-plus knots. All I can say is that casting a fly in winds of twenty knots is a real ball buster. On top of that, the boat launch was filled with big bass rigs. Huge horsepower-driven deals with gaudy coloring and logos of manufacturers plastered over the side, captained by men with giant belt buckles. These are the folks that inhabit one of the other "rooms" of fishing. We seldom think of each other. These guys all knew my guide. They would greet him then look at my fly-fishing setup and almost give him a pained look. Well, not almost.

Patrick F. McManus, the genius outdoor writer, once wrote a story called "A Fine and Pleasant Misery." My day in the Everglades was actually starting to take on proportions of that kind of misery.

All fishing has a pleasant element. At two o'clock, I told Rick that my day was done. We went back to the boat launch, which was adjacent to an Everglades tour business. You could, for a fee, take a tour aboard a giant airboat and see giant alligators. The one silver lining of the day was the hat I purchased. I like buying cool baseball caps and often fish in them. This one had a giant airboat and alligator embroidered on it. Very cool.

The next day I was to meet Rick behind the Macy's at the local mall. There was a spillway there with a crude boat launch cut into it. The thing about Florida is that if you want to build something you have to drain off the water, hence all the canals. The canals we were fishing were cut into ancient coral. A boater had to be careful of the steep, sharp side or risk ruining his boat through death of a thousand gouges.

We gingerly launched Rick's boat. As I was holding her away from sharp edges and waiting for Rick to park the truck, I was getting a new appreciation for his boat. He really thought it through. A big gaudy rig with too much size and power would compromise the fishing here. Luckily, Rick was secure in his masculinity and didn't have to compensate with a giant boat and matching horsepower.

As we were pulling away from Macy's, I noticed a stark difference from the fishing in the Blue Lagoon. This water was bluish-green and crystal clear, like a giant aquarium. The aquarium metaphor went well beyond the water; the canal was loaded with tons of aquarium fish. There were many kinds of cichlids (the family to which peacock bass belong). The brightest of them all was the red Midas cichlid. The day was cool and clear, which allowed you to see the fish a long way down. Rick thought it may have gotten too cool. I was thinking to myself that it was perfect. Sometimes a brief cooldown stirs things up. Turns out, I was correct.

I had purchased cheap polarized sunglasses sold in the fishing department at a discount store. They are about the best polarized glasses I have ever owned; they really allowed me to see what was going on below with almost total clarity, I switched over to a stouter set-up. I rigged up a 10-foot, 7-weight St. Croix Legend Elite rod with a G. Loomis Venture 7 reel. For some reason I just felt like I needed more strength. I shifted gears and tied on a smallish Clouser Minnow with silver and blue tones. It was smaller than Rick wanted me to fish. I tend to cast diminutive flies better than I do the larger counterparts. There is also an element of fear of nicking the rod with the bigger fly; that very circumstance is responsible for most of my rod breaks.

These canals were very different from the Blue Lagoon's. They were situated in a more upscale neighborhood, and the water appeared far "cleaner." The most dangerous things in water are the things you cannot see. It didn't take long that cool crisp morning to start connecting with nice peacock bass. They seemed to fight even harder on this cool morning, if that's possible.

At about this time I noticed a change in myself. I began to laugh and chortle and make other non-typical noises (for me at least). I was enjoying these fish immensely. They were beautiful, specked, eager, strong, aggressive fish of very good size. As humans, we like to qualify objects, and this fish was quickly rising up my favorite fish chart.

This particular set of canals also was really to my liking. Rick had noticed that the high winds and driving rain from the night before had blown much of the debris off the water. The water never had lots of debris but it did accumulate at the ends of some of the canals. As he noticed, he wondered about a certain canal that might be cleared out enough to fish. I always like when nature gives you a rare opportunity. In some of the Maine waters I fish, water level has the same effect. In some instances if the level is high enough, we can get into water that is usually inaccessible and the fishing can be very good. As I understand it, Rick was thinking it could be like that at the end of a couple canals.

As we pulled into secret canal number one, I could see a smile creep across Rick's face. We stopped at a place where there was a bird feeder hanging over the water. For whatever reason, underneath it was a large group of red midas cichlids. I began to cast to them and on the very first cast came a jarring strike. I set the hook and a few minutes later (and after a very respectable fight) I held in my hands one of those bright red fish. They are built much like a bluegill, and this guy had a big knot on his head and was obviously getting ready for love. I held him up to study him, in part because I had never caught one before. He was the size of a dinner plate and all of two pounds. I managed to catch four more under that bird feeder.

A little farther down we came to the end of the canal, which usually had a large mat of vegetative debris. But now it was completely clear. We could see numerous beds.

After hooking up with several nice fish I looked to the left. There was a very large peacock. We scrambled to get into position. Usually, pairs are associated with each bed. Sometimes it is just a male working on it but usually there are two. As I tossed the Clouser close, the big fish gulped the fly. It pulled so hard— the ten-foot rod was perhaps two feet shy of completing a circle. After some minutes, while trying to get a net under this prize, I happened to notice something from the corner of my eye. It was the other resident of that spawning bed. That other peacock bass was a fucking giant. At almost the same time, Rick saw the beast too.

Right then, we really meshed—having that rhythm you hope develops between client and guide. In a moment, I landed the large and belligerent peacock and set it back into the water.

Almost in one motion, Rick had the trolling motor swinging and retreating simultaneously. Bass guys are so good with those motors. His prowess made me feel pressure to keep up my end. On the second cast we had a hookup—a big peacock, which was going wherever the hell it wanted. His first run snagged the line in some brush along the bank. Rick was maneuvering the boat as I was trying to keep pressure on the fish. The line pulled from the brush and suddenly there was slack. I reeled fast. Real fast. I reeled fast enough to have tension on the fish again. He was headed to the large drainpipe nearby, and then around another smaller pipe. It was quite a busy ten minutes. Then Rick did manage to slip the net under the fish. It was nothing short of breathtaking. His weight came in just a hair under seven pounds. He was lit up in full spawning colors. In the next minutes we took photos and released the fish, and proceeded with high fives and whooping—honestly without any dignity whatsoever. It has been a long time since I celebrated like that. The only real question was: Why did it take me so long to find this?

We then went to the second canal that Rick had in mind. It was clear of debris as well. Even so, the dead end of that canal produced one nice peacock bass. By that time we had had a full day. As we were fishing our way back a big spray against the far bank caught our attention. It was a very big largemouth bass chasing a very stressed cichlid. We looked at each other and the newly well-oiled machine sprang into action. This bass was clearly over ten pounds. Rick began his boat handling and I started to cast. For several moments boat, line, bass and cichlid were flying every which way. At moments, it resembled a Benny Hill skit. We never came close to that fish. I can't even honestly tell you how the cichlid fared. We took a few moments to laugh and then just took a nice boat ride back. It was a great day and that was simply enough.

When we returned to the boat launch and trailered up the boat we had to discuss one thing. We had left the plans for the last day open. In the front seat of the truck, Rick started to laugh as he asked the question. "Where do you want to fish tomorrow?" I just smiled. We both knew that we would be coming right back here. The forecast was for a very similar day; the only real difference was that it would be five or six degrees warmer. The place was on fire. My only regret was that tomorrow was the final day.

As I was driving to meet Rick at the rendezvous spot, my mind was finally putting some of this into order. Some of it still defied falling neatly into the cubicles I like my life to fall into. Like crumbs on a bed sheet, it was annoying. In a way, it felt a little inappropriate—I was clearly in a place that I was not meant to be. If it was kosher then why had I not come across another fly rod in almost a week? Worse yet I was loving the hell out of this.

I kept thinking about it in these terms, and of that movie *Blue Lagoon* which had a theme of forbidden love. I was participating in this peacock thing where the bait dunkers crinkled their noses when they saw me. I knew guys like Ted Williams would hate the invasive species part of this. Sorry Ted, but these guys are where they belong. Sometimes things aren't right in the beginning, like people born the wrong gender. The peacock bass here just seem to fit. Past the invasive side, I am sure that fly guys overlook this fish because they feel it is beneath them. That's ok—there is more for me. It was at about this thought that I arrived behind Macy's. This mental reconciliation would have to wait.

I greeted Rick and commented how the day was even nicer than the day before. I said to him "I bet we can have a twenty-five fish day." He smiled and said, "That would be awesome, especially with the fly rod."

Rick had held that it was much more challenging to catch these guys with a fly rod. It was one of those mornings that just felt good. We were both well sharpened and well patterned by the previous day's fishing. The action started early and fish were eager. We went in a different direction, and this day would take us past a park where Rick had made friends with a duck with crazy feathers on its head. He was telling me about it as we approached the park. Sure enough, there was a big white duck with a Mohawk.

The day just kept getting better. There was a spot where we spied a bed with two healthy peacock bass. As I hooked the first one, I heard a crazy sound behind me. I turned my head and right there feeding in the yard we were fishing next to was a flock of peacocks. So here I was with a hard fighting peacock bass on my line in the middle of a flock of peacocks. You can't make this shit up. Luckily, we had taken a few photos on our phone. After we landed the fish I looked at Rick. "Did you know they would be here?"

Rick kept laughing. "In all my years guiding here I have never seen that before!" I was convinced that it must be some kind of omen. Of what, I still don't have any idea.

The highlight of the day was that one of the canals opened up into a small lake. The lake was completely surrounded by upscale homes. Almost the whole shoreline was sand beaches. In fact, the whole lake bottom was soft material. With most of the waterway being hard coral, this lake and its soft bottom was rare and perfect bedding. The bottom looked very similar to a honeycomb. There were beds upon beds. The bedding was not segregated in any way; all species were mixed together. It didn't take long to pattern the peacocks.

There was another lake similar to this lake. It was just a little farther. The fishing there was even better. As we approached a retaining wall that was lit by a light post, we saw him. It was a huge peacock. We cast to him for over a half hour. It was certain that he had been seen by others. No matter how deftly I casted, no matter how softly the cast lilted upon the water, he spooked with each one. This fish was 12–14 pounds and easily the Florida record. Rick mentioned that he sees a few of these every year. I can tell you that the record book really is meaningless to me. On the other hand, big fish get the testosterone flowing. I had caught big fish here, and I had casted to record fish here. I couldn't help it, I was just digging this fishery.

The sun started to hang lower. As in every trip, the end comes. It was a great day. We caught and landed thirty-one fish, twenty-six of which were peacocks. Rick said this was one of his best days with or without a fly rod. I like a seasoned guide who knows how to get a tip. It would take about forty minutes to get back to the launch, and my mind picked up where it left off in the car. What had I done?

I have to be honest" I had fallen in love. Did I like this more than my beloved brook trout? What about my lifelong thing with smallmouth bass? I don't know exactly where it all stacks up in my heart. This feels a little naughty—like forbidden love. That feeling makes me love it all the more. What do you want from a guy who still wears tie-dye?

I booked a whole week with Rick next year.

The Zen of Home Water

Out beyond the ideas of wrongdoing
and right doing there is a lake.
I'll meet you there.

When the soul lies down in that water
the world is too full to talk about.

—*Rumi*

If ever you spend enough time in nature and with a rod in hand, you develop a beat—a collection of water that you fish over and over again. The place where you develop enough familiarity that you know and understand nuances that are not immediately understood by someone who spends less time there. It is in this familiarity that we come to understand and have an affinity for these places. These are our home waters.

In my life I have been lucky to have two areas that feel like home. In the first instance, I spent most of my life living on the south shore of Lake Ontario. To call it a lake is a little misleading. A lake is something you can swim across. Lake Ontario has been crossed by swimmers, but only by well-trained and seasoned athletes. If I did it, most of the distance would be a postmortem float. In reality, it is an inland freshwater sea. The web of life that it captures is enormous. For the better part of a half century, I have tried to get to know her and the water that flows to her. In many places, I have gotten to know and feel the life force it exerts. I am not the only one. On a fall day fishing Oak Orchard River, I share the experience with many others. Each of us is trying to find a little piece of water to enjoy and *feel*. Often, there is a collective joy.

My other home waters happened more subtly. It was a gradual seduction. Trip after trip to the north woods of Maine eased the area into my DNA. Coy and difficult, she took many years to get to know. Over time, she was a slow siren that now has me completely. The area around Grand Lake Stream does not have the powerful web of life that my other home water does. It is easy to see the contrast. Lake Ontario houses major cities—Buffalo, Rochester, and Toronto. Then there are many smaller places. Life and civilization thrives on its shores. Grand Lake Stream is lucky to have three hundred year-round residents.

In the thought process of having two home ranges, I began to think—of all the water in my home ranges, which one is *the* one? At first you think they all are. This is complete bullshit. Like saying a parent loves all their children the same. You love them all but one reflects you like no other. It is a type of self-confrontation we tend to avoid. It lacks a certain political correctness. We are conditioned to be judicious and diplomatic. It becomes ingrained to the point where I have to remove layers of veneer to examine the simple question—what is the one water that reflects me? The realization that societal programming is so deep pisses me off.

In reviewing all the water, I thought I knew who she was. There is a lake in Washington County, Maine. She is not very large. You could swim across her. I could relate to her past. In the beginning she was something else. She was clean and pure. Brook trout and salmon teemed in her clear, cool water. Then she was assaulted. Big corporations logged the rich forest around her. The locals fished the delicious and seemingly endless bounty of trout and salmon. In an event all too familiar in that era—she collapsed. All that was left were a few white perch and chain pickerel. The wildlife that visited the lake did not come back.

Nature abhors voids. In time, niches demand to be filled. I am a big believer of the Gaia hypothesis. It is the simple proposition that organisms interact with their inorganic surroundings on Earth to form a self-regulating, complex system that contributes to keeping the conditions for life on the planet. Very Zen—and in this case, this means smallmouth bass. Smallmouth fill the niche and flourish. Not the same paradigm as before, but a thriving and invigorating one. The lake had an abundance of large smallmouth bass that ate willingly. The word was out that the lake was back.

Humans, being slow learners, for the second time, destroyed a beautiful fishery. The bass went. The lake was a husk again. In harsh lessons, some do learn. There were a few like-minded conservationists who had the lake deemed a no-kill lake and then began restocking it with bass taken from lakes with abundances. The bass took hold and the web of life returned to the lake. In the years since, people noticed that the bass were not as big as before. The bass that were planted from the "abundant" lakes ended up with genetics that filled the carrying capacity of those lakes with smaller bass and fewer bigger ones. So this lake, I will call it Zen Lake, is full of smallmouth bass between two and three pounds.

In my mind, I felt that Zen Lake was my one true home water. Like Walden for Thoreau, did this lake help me to live deliberately? I needed to find out for sure. It had been nearly a year since I was there. My life had its complications and they kept me away. I had recovered from a harsh battle with cancer. I was in the finishing phases of rebuilding a life. In the confrontation with death, I was forced to re-examine who and what I was. I needed to get back to my lake to see if it indeed was my one true home water.

In the time of planning, I could see that my return was going to be early August, well past the glory of May and June bass on spawning beds. In those times, catching hundreds of fish on top-water flies is possible. August can be hot and moody. The one thing is for sure—the bass showing up will be prime. They will be the ones that survived the spawn and predators, becoming top-shelf predators themselves, feeding and preparing for the Maine winter. In the process, they become hard and strong. They offer a fight more vicious than the spawning version of themselves just months earlier. These are the smallmouth we remember best.

In my time off from fishing, I began to search for the lesser-loved bamboo-rod makers. It is easy to know that a Winston or Payne bamboo will be a thing of beauty. I wanted to find the lesser-known gems. In the past I had fished with a Genesee Valley rod. The maker was a guy named Joe Perrigo. He was a local maker. I never got to know him and he made a few rods for a short time. The rod I tried was a friend's. It was as smooth and lovely as any I have held. Though it was made practically under my nose in my region, I am still looking for one. The lesson is that there are some fine rods being made by fine artists, though they lack high budgets for promoting and selling their rods. The thought that there are great rods out there I don't even know about drives me nuts.

You have to spend lots of time scouring the internet for these guys. Then you have to be willing to take a chance. I won't lie—I have purchased some rods that were awful. The makers followed some formula and missed the art of rod building altogether.

After being off my home waters for some time, I wanted to find a rod for the occasion. In life, if we marry fine things with fine moments, so we can create personal historic memories. Wine can be like that. In fact, I find an easy parallel between the crafting of fine wines and fine bamboo rods.

In my process, I look for a maker who has some experience. Then you try to find some reviews or comments. The biggest part of it is the phone call. It is amazing how much you can learn about a person in a simple conversation. In this process, I talked to a charming southern gentleman named Jim Mills. The conversations were thoughtful and humble. I instinctively understood he was an artist. He had made fly rods out of bamboo for a long time. I had never heard of Raven Fork Rods, and was determined to order one. I settled on a 5-weight with a Granger taper. I told him I wanted light blue guide wrappings. He asked, "Carolina Blue?"

"Sure," I said, chuckling to myself because he was from North Carolina. With his Southern twang, Carolina Blue sounded perfect. Perhaps six weeks later the rod arrived, following a phone call from Jim in which he had expressed some reservations on the way the colors came together on the light bamboo rod. He offered to rewrap it without cost if I didn't love it.

The package came and I anxiously opened it. I put the rod together and held it in my hands. I smiled a broad smile; the rod felt good. I looked at the color for a while. It grew on me the same way a pretty girl with a sexy gap between her teeth can grow on you when she smiles. In time, I could see myself loving her. I loaded her with a Cortland Classic 444 DT5F and she cast like a dream. We expect amazing rods to come out of the West and even the Northeast. Seldom do you hear of one coming from the south. In retrospect, it is the perfect location for a "sleeper" rod builder. It would be a short time till I could get my Carolina Blue rod on the water. The front lawn (for casting practice) is one thing; the angry maw of a bruiser bass is another.

The trip to Maine has remained the same 750 miles it always was, but I am not the same man I always was. In my youth, I would throw a bunch of gear in the vehicle and drive off. Most times I would leave early in the morning and tear it off in one day. Sometimes I would leave the evening before so I would be able to arrive to fish the following morning. There are days I miss that version of me. Now, the trip is far more deliberate. I take greater care in packing, since forgetting something could be problematic. I tend to make the journey in two days. I am still as anxious as ever to get there, but limitations of the flesh are part of the aging process. There always seem to be tradeoffs. While the younger version of me could rip through the trip quickly, he needed to. My present version has the luxury of being deliberate. Young, anxious, and limited versus older, deliberate, and unlimited. Which one is better? I can't say. I am glad I get to be both.

It was early evening when Louie pulled up trailing my Grand Laker Canoe. Louie is a Maine Guide, a camp caretaker and, most importantly, a friend. He would paddle my canoe while I'd cast from the bow. I got into the truck and we made our way to Zen Lake. Usually, I like to pay attention to the ride out to the lake. On this trip, I was preoccupied with the notion of spending time on the lake. You think your home water will welcome you back with open arms. The process can be fickle. The rule in life is that things change and nothing remains constant. The possibility exists that the home lake will have changed so much that it will lose that familiar feeling. The trip to the lake was one of wondering how I still fit into its soul and it into mine.

That first evening was cool and clear. The smell and sound of the place was familiar. As I lay cast after cast upon the water, my soul began to open up. The fishing that night was wonderful. My casts with the new rod were soft and crisp. Takes were sharp and brisk. The fights were tenacious and frequent. It seemed like I had just left here. I told Louie I wanted to come back again tomorrow. He looked at me for a moment and agreed. It has always been our tradition to rotate lakes. Visiting our favorites more often than the rest but seldom if ever repeating. I think Louie understood and acquiesced in a move that was sensitive and understanding. Emotions are rarely shared between us.

The following evening was a bit more humid, bordering on muggy. The weather had been frequently changing and was clearing off in its latest mood. The fishing was off but just as sweet. In the corner of a south bay was a cow moose feeding peacefully with her calf. It was a rare gift and something I had never seen on my lake. Moments later the sound of heaving wings pushing downdrafts of air made me turn to regard a mature bald eagle. He landed in a large spruce and returned my stare. It was clear that the karma of the evening had seen fit to send him as the welcoming committee. I was on my home water. There was no doubt. As I was thinking this, a loon's cry echoed across the lake. Many have given special and spiritual meaning to the sound of a loon's cry. These particular loons are part clown and part thug. I have known this pair for a long time. In the moment after they recognized me, they began swimming around my boat. Looking at me with one eye and then the other, with a "where have you been" look. This was followed by the "I hope you can still catch fish" look that one loon gives to another after they had not seen each other for a while. They remembered all the bass I begrudgingly released to them in past years. It was not long after that they were full on easy meals begrudgingly released to them again. Maybe just a little less begrudged. Full and sassy, they resumed their calls. I thought I could detect some joy in them, that they were glad to see me again.

I think Louie was a little surprised when I said I wanted to fish there again the following night. He witnessed the welcome I was given by the loons. All things coming together in a special way could only be interpreted as a confirmation. Again he shook his head and we agreed to fish the following evening.

The next day, shortly after we launched the canoe, the weather became ominous. The weather for the last three days had been only volatile. I will risk many things—there are days on which I just won't wear a seatbelt, or I'll talk to strangers—but I don't fuck around with lightning. Sitting in a boat with a rod in your hand during a lightning storm is crazy. With lightning heading our way, and no chance to make it back to the launch, we had to find shelter.

I pointed to the old camp at a nearby point, and we worked our way there quickly. As we landed the canoe on the beach, an older man walked down to greet us.

"Hey, Louie," the man called.

"Hey, Jack," Louie replied. "Do you mind if we hang out here until the storm passes?"

Of course not, was the answer. Louie introduced me and we were invited to sit on Jack's porch well nestled in the trees on the point. The camp was obviously very old. I listened to Louie and Jack catch up. As I listened, their Down East accents seemed to thicken by the minute. I felt like I was stuck in one of those old Pepperidge Farm commercials. In reality, it was two North Woods guys reaffirming their chosen life. To talk that way among themselves was to identify a connection between them with an outdoor life that went back generations. As the conversation turned to me, I was given the history of the 105-year old camp. Nestled in the pines, you could watch the storm rage—but I was dry on that porch. It was a beautiful storm.

Old Jack told about how his great grandfather built the camp. How he would guide sports fishing and hunting to make ends meet. He told of the camp's history with the lumber people. Jack clasped his hands together and made a loon call. Much to my amazement the loons started to come closer and began calling back. I had the sense my loons weren't as much mine as I had previously thought. (You really can never trust loons.) The old stories piled up in number and intensity. The last story was about a guy who had a wife who was a schoolteacher. It turned out she was spending too much time in the principal's office. At some point, the husband caught on. In his anger, he managed to catch the principal "visiting" his wife at his house in town. The husband decided to hold the naked principal at gunpoint in front of the picture window. It was quite a standoff. The principal without principles was eventually negotiated out of his jam. Events like that fade very slowly from the local memory.

Then Louie and Jack started tracing back their North Woods heritage until they had family members in common. Like fourth cousins and great uncles. This usually is a signal that the visit is winding down. They had noticed the storm had passed. The recounting is a segue to ending a visit. It also serves as an inventory to who is still here and who has passed away. Best regards are given and the parties stand up to prepare the final goodbye. It is a polite and pleasant goodbye.

We were out on the water again, the storm still visible and heading north. The weather that followed it was cool and kind. You could feel the slightest hint of autumn. The height of summer passed with that storm. The wind cycled down and as the sun went low in the sky the horizon was filled with golden pink and purple hues. It was calming. The fishing was coming on as the light level kept falling. At some point, we began to work our way back to the boat launch. (We call it that, but it is actually a spot worn flat from our launches over time.) The moon was rising and almost full. In that brief interlude when the last rays of sunlight intertwine with the bright moonlight, we startled a beaver. It gave that signature tail slap on the water. The loud noise made me jump. After being startled, my senses were heighted. I could hear and see all the little cues.

Wide eyed, I picked up some commotion in the shallows next to the boat launch. I aimed a popper at the spot. In a moment, it went under and I set the hook. The large predator tore off for deeper water. In another moment, the line broke off. It was a big fish. Bigger than we ever guessed was in this water. I didn't mind. In a short while we were setting the canoe on its trailer. The sun's retreat was now complete. The day was done and all that was left was the ride back to the cabin.

The ride on the bumpy dirt road gave me time to think of living as it was. I knew almost instantly on that first day that this was my home water. I spent the next three days basking in reaffirmation. We have no choice; we must cross into the future. The best we can hope for is to take some of the greater things forward with us. In this place, Zen Lake, I can feel deep inside that I belong to it and it belongs to me, that our life forces comingle and seem to dwell with each other. In that way, our stories intertwine across history.

Sunfish and Strawberry Wine

> One should always be drunk. That's all that
> matters. . . . But with what? With wine,
> with poetry, or with virtue, as you choose.
> But get drunk.
>
> —*Charles Baudelaire*

One of the greatest joys of living in the Northeast is the advent of the seasons. All four hold their wonders, each giving what it can and then, at just the right moment, giving way to the next. I can qualify my love of each. In studying the rite of spring, the stirring of the bounty in the earth is truly arousing. The early flowers—crocuses and daffodils—wake up and tell of warmer, lighter days ahead.

In fly-fishing, we have serious business and then we have nonsense. My nature is drawn to nonsense like a moth to a bug light. (Fooled you, I didn't say flame! See, nonsense.) Sometimes, subjects don't have to mean anything more than what they are. My spring trips to Pine Lake are just like that. To take a whimsical trip, with a perky little 3-weight, in search of delicious colorful slabs of bluegills and sunfish.

Pine Lake is small—really, it's a pond. A lovely late-stage eutrophic lake, its better days are behind it. It once gave up good largemouth bass. Now you must release them, as the fertile lake is slowly dying. It is a natural cycle. As the conditions have become worse for the bass, they have got better for the panfish. You could say Pine Lake has become the perfect domain for the bluegill and sunfish that live there. They have waited out their queue and are finally at the front of the line. There are a few places on the lake where they spawn but most of the action takes place on the southern shore. One stretch about 75 yards long consists of a sandy gravel perfect for bedding during the spawn.

The peak of the spawn seems to slide playfully around, demanding you to keep it under observation. I knew I would be close to arriving at the right time. I had the cooler in the old Sears johnboat that I borrow when I fish the lake. The oars are old and weathered; the paddle section has worn thin over time. No motors are allowed on Pine Lake. The thought of one would be obscene.

The brass oarlocks rhythmically knocking in the socket keep time with your progress across the lake. In front of me is a cooler filled with ice and a bottle of strawberry wine—Boone's Farm Strawberry Hill. No pretense here—a fruity, cheap wine with a kick. Buried deep in the ice. It needs to be just this side of a brain freeze to be right. The day is a perfect mile-high blue sky. As the rhythm of the oarlocks carries me closer to where I want to fish, I smell the smell.

It is such a wonderful smell. It is briny, fishy, laden with a certain saltiness. It is the smell of sex. No matter how old a buck I become, I will always know that smell. It is as primal as the earth itself. It lets me know it is going to be all right. That it is a full orgasmic, contentious orgy happening straight ahead. Though you could take a thermometer to see if the water temperature has triggered the pretty round fish to get ready for love, there is no need. All you need is a clear nose.

As you get closer, you can see the spawn beds jammed together. It has the look of an underwater honeycomb. The smaller fish are risking it in the shallower water. At any moment, a great Blue Heron could swoop in and make vacancies. If the fish were bigger, they could fight for the prime real estate. Still, they are all busy jockeying for the best spot. The gods have them needing to breed. They don't even notice the large shadow approaching. They may hear the oars *swish, swish, swish, swish.* No matter, they have to concentrate on the task at hand.

I know I am the only guy who comes and takes fish here. It isn't that it is private. Though the lakeshore is, the fishing is open to the public. One of the requirements is that you sign in. I can see from the books I am the only fisherman since my last visit, before the spawn. At the sign-in book, I run into the caretaker. He tells me to please take as many as I can. The panfish are of a good size. Some of the regulars who had fished in seasons past have been conspicuously missing. I wonder if one day, when I am missing, will anyone fish this place? Fly fishing is a sport that has grown up. It has so many glamorous components I have to wonder if this panfishing is too pedestrian, anymore. It doesn't matter. I am here and I love it. I tie on a size 12 Bluegill Bee. It doesn't matter. The fish don't remember the flies and would knock the shit out of anything I tied on.

I am wrong—it does matter to me. I want the fly to be right.

I run my finger down the delicate spine of the 3-weight. One of the qualities of genius of a premier fly-rod maker is finding the spine to the rod correctly. It is surely more art than science. A master craftsman will sometimes contemplate a subtle spine. In the end, the wood tells the maker just what the rod will be. It is one of the reasons I love bamboo. You can take two rods made by the same guy in the same way and they can have personalities as different as daughters. In this way, we certainly love them all but the glory of finding one that suits you is special. Rods that love you back and just work better with the way you fish—this 3-weight is like that. It is sweet and it is delicate. Sometimes I am afraid to fish her. Bamboo is sturdy but not tough. I am close with some guys who own historical rods. They wear gloves when handling them. I do respect their delicacy, and the history of the grand sport. I just can't own a rod I won't fish. In time I think I will. I have even retired a rod. "Jerry's Killer" is a custom-made 7-weight from Carl Coleman. I have caught thousands of fish with it, including some very large ones. When I hold the rod it feels tired. Rods are like prize fighters; they have only so many fights in them. The number, exactly, is not known, but you can tell when it's getting close. I know Carl's rod will never fight another round so it sits in my cabinet.

The 3-weight is lovely and game. She can sport a perfect parabolic arc. One of the great things about fly-fishing is choosing the rod weight. You can handicap the game to keep it in proper proportions. A 3-weight on a scrappy bluegill approaching three-quarters of a pound would need to be handled similarly to a big Atlantic salmon on a stout 8-weight. It is the proportions that keep the sport lively. Life and fly fishing mirror each other. Perhaps that is why I enjoy it so. Life without proportion is wrong. Fly fishing without proportion is wrong too. The deftness we apply to both is directly related to the joy we take.

The sweet little rod and the light leader deliver the fly delicately. The tiny ripples caused by the fly push out concentrically. It is enough to gather the intended response. In a moment, the fight is on. The round fish use their shape to best advantage, keeping their side to you, forcing you to work them. Hard pulling, with the fish swimming in tighter and tighter circles. Eventually I reach into the water and extract a fat male bluegill. He is easily as big as my hand, that is the benchmark. He will go into the cooler. There are many fish here. Each cast elicits attention. Though there is no limit, I tell myself I will keep forty; that is enough for a nice fish fry. When I was younger I enjoyed fileting fish. I could spend hours doing it. Now, forty is the arbitrary number with which I close the deal. The knock on bluegill and sunfish is that they are too boney for eating. That is a myth. They are about as easy a fish to filet as there is. I'm guessing where the rumor started there was a hell of a honey hole.

The sun is bright and direct, with no sign of any clouds to divert some of its powerful rays. I could feel my core heating up. I know that taking sun like that is probably not a good idea. It felt good. We have put ourselves in the position where we take calculated risks just to enjoy the planet, as our species always had. This is the position we created when we evolved to the point of imposing our own paradigms on our planet. You have to wonder if that kind of evolution is a *cul de sac*. There are times when I choose to live in the moment. I slathered on sunscreen and wore a hat. I thought maybe the other guys that used to fish here were killed off by the sun. I laughed to myself at the silly notion. I am enjoying this.

The direct sun has another effect—it can make you thirsty. I sit down on the bench seat and open the cooler. I look at the eight big panfish lying on the ice. Quickly, I figured I was 20 percent done. My mind does that, always chugging along and redefining things. Then I stick my hand into the ice. The chill sends goose bumps across my body. At the same time, a warmish breeze blows across my stooped back. It's great to be alive. I reach for the bottle of wine I know is there. As the sting from the cold starts, I find the bottle. I retrieve it and shake off the ice chips. With my right hand, I grab the screw cap. With enough force, I turn it so the cap breaks from the security ring. *Crack, crack, crack, crack*—we all know the sound of a screw top breaking loose. I tip up the bottle to my lips and take a deep drink. As the sweet wine hit my taste buds, the cold water from the outside of the bottle runs down my chin and then my shirt. After a deep pull, I wipe my mouth with my shirt sleeve and make an audible *ahhh* that travels in a satisfying way across the water.

It is delicious. Not the wine but the day *and* the wine. I had never had Boone's Farm Strawberry Hill before. It was on the shelf at the store at which I always stop before I fish Pine Lake. In the years of my college education, I would purchase some sour apple flavor from the great Boone's Farm. It was affordable and somewhat tasty in the same way you can enjoy a Charm's Blow Pop. At $3.99 in the store by Pine Lake, the intrigue was too great and the nostalgic pull tickled my fancy. It was one of the better impulse buys I have made.

Sitting there in the sun, drinking ice-cold strawberry wine on Pine Lake, was delicious. Delicious moments in life seldom have any weight to them. They occur on a whim and tickle your fancy. They are fleeting and unpredictable. You just have to enjoy and be amazed. Like a meteor shower, or a rainbow. Fragile, lovely, and short-lived.

It was the hottest part of the day. That time just before three when the constant sun and its warming effect has slowed things down a bit. I was still catching fish and was approaching the self-imposed limit.

I lifted the lid of the cooler. I had culled a nice batch of fish so far. Next to them was the half-empty bottle of wine. It was a good day at a good pace. I had switched to a blue popper. All the action was chewing up flies. In a mildly buzzed mindset I decided a more durable fly would be better. The nice thing about panfish on poppers is the sound of the take. Like an over-articulated kiss. *SMACK!* Then you set the hook. This smack had me set up on a very good fish. He instantly put a hard arc into the rod. I had a few like that that day. You suddenly pay closer attention because you want to protect the delicate rod. The fish was pulling hard. You could feel the constant and rhythmic thrusts of the fish's tail. Each flex of the muscle sent vibration up the line, through the rod, and into me.

It was not a great, epic fight. Well, that is not right. . . as all things are relevant in their own way. The fish had big heart and fought his best fight. The duration was no longer than four or five minutes. The best fight of the day and I loved it.

When I pulled the fish from the water, he was a very large sunfish. Maybe he weighed as much as a pound. I suspect a little less. A magnificent bull. He was mature and had the slight head bulge the dominant males would get. His colors were in full spawning electrification. The blues and green were intermingled with yellows and oranges. He was just so colorful even by sunfish standards. His belly was that creamy orange you get from the freshest farm eggs.

I took the popper out of his mouth and set him on the ice. He lay there with his gills fanning, alongside the half-drunk bottle. I looked at the fish, along with the rest, he was so much more striking. The thought in my mind was "Too pretty to kill." I carefully picked him off the ice and revived him in the water. With a flick of his tail he was gone. It made me smile.

I sat down and took a break. With the bottle in my hand, I took it all in. About 30 yards away, I could see a muskrat working on his summer home. Perched in a tree nearby was a male cardinal calling its distinct "birdie, birdie, birdie." The sound of the wind blowing through the freshly greened boughs of the trees. It was a good day. I never was taken into my backing. I was never bothered by another human being. The sweet strawberry taste was as good as any expensive Riesling I had ever purchased, thus confirming what I had always known: the magic of wine, and wine is magic, is matching the wine to the surroundings.

This is not an epic tale, by any means. In fish-story importance, it even lacks the required stretching of the truth. For me, it is the subtle essence of this sport of ours. Some truths were found that day that probably have no applicable life lessons. One that comes to mind is: What kind of wine goes with sunfish? Then there are others that teach that the greatness of life isn't necessarily the big life altering events. Instead, it is the small unpretentious moments that give us fleeting tastes of simple pleasures. One of those little moments is a tale about sunfish and strawberry wine.

That's Entertainment and the San Juan Special

A sirens scream upon the silver screen and
you can't look away. That's entertainment.

It could be a common perception—that being in the management of a major entertainer was some kind of glamorous, elite life. I have to admit that my almost thirty years on the road with George Carlin had some of that. Times like being special guest at the Rose Bowl game after the parade had some great associated memories. Those kinds of special show-biz moments were very cool. The reality was that those moments were few and far between. For most of those years, ours was one of the hardest working acts in the business.

Most years, we would have performances totaling more than two hundred days. If you add travel time, you were never home. The rule of thumb was travel to the city, get to the show hall and set up, run the performance while taking care of all the business in that short window, and then leave to do it all over again the next day. People would often ask where we were the night before and I would need to pull the schedule out to tell them. In the course of a tour, nights and theatres and hotels blend together.

It is a life that is hard on body and mind. You find out exactly what your constitution is made of. The close quarters and endless hours you spend with people are telling. In the end you develop a certain road-tested closeness. I mean, how many White Castle burgers can you share with someone before a bond develops? The White Castle burger is a show business staple; just mention the word "slider" to someone in the industry and they will smile knowingly. It is a part of the culture. You are moving late at night, long after all the people who have enjoyed the show are gone. You need to cover ground so you can get to the next night's show. This often leaves you at the mercy of the road and her cuisine. If we stayed in a place more than one night and could actually sit and enjoy a dinner—well, that was special.

It was not only solid show after show. Typically, we played Thursday, Friday, Saturday, and Sunday. Sometimes we had a Wednesday show, but usually we had at least two days off in a week. If you could get home, that was great; if not, you worked your way to the next leg of the tour. This is when I would scheme to fish. My strategy was to look at maps and find routes to see where I needed to be in order to fish a day or two. Sometimes we would be interrupted by acts of God. For the most part, these were weather-related and we mostly dreaded them. It usually meant squeezing in the show at a later date in a way that didn't make any geographic sense.

There is some truth to everything being bigger in Texas. When we toured Texas, it usually took two weeks and often we would forgo the usual days off. I enjoyed Texas and its people. They are warm and hospitable. The only way Texas sucks is if you are on death row. The state rivals some of the Islamic fundamentalist regimes in the pace of their executions. They think it helps, but science and statistics say otherwise. The idea has to do with a large fundamental Christian population. I just cannot understand how a religion whose center figure was a man who preached "love your neighbor as yourself" and forgiveness, and who eventually died from execution, could favor execution. That irony aside, I like Texas.

One of the other factors about Texas that you have to watch is the weather. It was hurricane season one of the years we were there in the 1990s. I am not sure exactly who noticed that a hurricane could come into play. It was already a brutal tour. Nerves and tempers were wearing thin. I remember the feeling shared by everyone, including George, hoping the weather would knock us off track, like children praying for a snow day. It was a selfish prayer. It had no malice. Our secret prayer was that those dates would be cancelled for safety's sake and that the hurricane would travel benignly onward. We kept a watchful eye as the dates approached and the hurricane grew stronger. The cancelation of concert dates is a dull and complicated process. It finally came to zero hour and it looked bad. It was what we wished for but not how we wished it might occur. It was coming inland and people—millions of people—were taking evacuation routes.

As the complexities of cancelling a leg of a tour came together, Dave and I were just entering Texas. I would often drive along the tour if I could—Ford Broncos in the early years, then Ford Excursions; I found them a comfortable and safe way to go. Over the years, I would hire drivers and really pile up the miles. During this time the driver was Dave, not me. We were sitting in a rest area in east Texas while I was burning up my cell phone. Finally, the Texas leg would be rescheduled. Dave and I had roughly ten days to get to the next gig in Arizona. We decided that we could get a nice room, form a strategy, and go with the flow. The first part was to get just outside of the evacuation area and stop.

There are a lot of people in Texas. When all of them decide to leave, rooms become scarce. We would stop and be told the same old story. All the rooms were sold out because of the hurricane. Eventually we wound up exhausted and near Roswell, New Mexico. Normally this would be considered a sleepy little Western town. Something had happened outside of Roswell just after World War II—extraterrestrials crash landed near there. At least that's what the U.S. Army said, until they changed their minds. Then the government altered its version of the story about every decade, just enough to keep the conspiracy folks fully charged.

In my mind, the real conspiracy is—why? To keep an economic pulse in a little tiny place like Roswell? Anyway, landing there was fun. Dave and I spent the better part of the day looking around and traveling the E.T. highway, buying funny little men t-shirts, mugs, and even little men dolls. I still have one wearing a 10-gallon hat. I don't know why but the thought of a civilization travelling millions of light years to get a cowboy hat just fucking kills me.

After a day playing the part of conspiracy tourist, I was ready to find some fish. I called an old fishing friend of mine who had relocated West one state at a time. I thought he might have a suggestion. He was tickled I was in Roswell and said he needed me to send him a coffee mug. Then he said there was a good fly shop in Taos. He reminded me that I should chill there for a bit. That the place was full of "our people."

Our people were the remnants of the counterculture and their disciples, although *disciple* is probably the wrong word. I mean those who came too late for the 1960s but still wanted to taste the free-thinking, coexisting lifestyle. I am not sure if they ever can get it. I hope they can.

We finished up our lunch at the Little Ale Inn and made tracks for Taos. I was secretly amused. I knew that for Dave and his blue-collar mindset, he was going from one alien landscape to another.

Taos, New Mexico, is a great place. The remnants of the counter-culture era are as strong there as anywhere. Everywhere you look, the roots of the Beat Generation show through. It is an artistic place where spirits run free, where owning the disposable-razor franchise would be a losing proposition. A place where subversive thoughts and creativity prevail. The harmless kind that make people smile. The writers D. H. Lawrence and Willa Cather and photographers Georgia O'Keeffe and Ansel Adams lived there; the actor Dennis Hopper lived there for decades.

As I pulled up to the Taos fly shop, out front was the coolest VW bus I had ever seen. It was some kind of hybrid Grateful Dead tour/fly-fishing bus. It had symbols of both pursuits painted all over the sides. Inside the fly shop were several types of people. I am a people watcher and observing the culture is a hobby. Clearly, different people were here. You could see that fly fishing had recently sprawled across many demographics. I was familiar with the old guard but times were changing. I was holding my breath with all the other dinosaurs.

It has been almost twenty years since then. The movie *A River Runs Through It* sparked a major influx into the sport. Before the movie, fly fishing was a fringe affair but the players were a fairly homogenous, quirky, lovable bunch. During the influx, which was happening about the time I was in Taos, big money entered the sport. It changed fly fishing forever. Like almost anything, some of that was good, some of it not so good. The guys who were around before the change lament the loss of the close-knit family feel. That was a major loss that we will probably never quite get back. On the other side of the coin, the industry gained clout. The money has engendered some nice equipment, albeit at a price that makes the fly-fishing "elders" struggle. The best result is that the environmental arm of fly fishing is now able to flex more muscle. Some pretty little pockets of genetic diversity would have disappeared without this help.

The man at the fly shop sold me some flies and gave me some tips on where they would work in the area. I am sure he saw my New York plates. I knew then and there the spots he bird-dogged me to were the standard ones. Those streams and rivers that show up on the fish-and-wildlife websites. There would be no chance of me hitting anyone's honey hole.

I enjoyed the fishing. The endless sunshine was a treat for a guy used to the dark, moody weather of Central New York. The "stocked" streams the man at the fly shop directed me to were pleasant, as well. I was managing about a dozen 12- to 16-inch trout a day, and various smaller ones. This was good fishing for anyone. In the back of my mind, though, I kept thinking about how close the San Juan was. It is one of those places that has become legendary. If a flyfisherman has to have a bucket list, the San Juan should be on it.

I don't like the idea of a bucket list. It is too yuppied out. I prefer life at its unscripted best. There are those who feel they have to control every aspect of their lives, even the things they would like to do before they die. What if you died with only half the list done? Does that mean your life missed the mark? Would you have to come back and finish it in your next life? I suppose if I have one—a bucket list—it only has one item: live well today.

I know we like to think we have more control in life than we actually do, but if you can manage to live well today, you are doing good. The philosophical tap dancing aside, the San Juan was close and it seemed to compel me to try it. I had been reading about it for many years. I turned to Dave and told him, "Tomorrow we head to the San Juan." I'm not sure this meant much to him. Dave, although a dependable driver, was not an angler.

My first impressions of the San Juan were not very good. It was at first light and I was rigged up with the "worm"—a San Juan Worm. I thought it was fitting, that my first cast should be with that fly. No one warned me it would be combat fishing.

There are few things I dislike more than combat fishing—a dentist with a bent drill bit and women who have lipstick on their teeth are the only two I can think of right off. There is a difference between crowded conditions and combat fishing. The latter usually sees someone needing a hook removed from a body part at some point. The snagging for salmon on Great Lakes tributaries was my first exposure to combat fishing. I would go down to the bridge at the Genesee River and watch, somewhat amused, and literally above it all on the bridge and therefore safe. This was the first time I had witnessed that kind of aggression from my brethren. People were walking over and casting over each other's lines. Some were chasing big and visibly harassed fish. It was a sure departure from the genteel roots of the sport. Fly fishing always evoked a simple spirit that was in touch with sentiments like Thoreau's *Life in the Woods*. If someone on the Genesee River tried communing with nature, he would have been stomped. Clearly this was different than in the *Field & Stream* articles.

I took a second look at the San Juan situation and noticed some sports were fishing from drift boats. It looked better than wading; you could keep a civilized air about you. I decided I would hire a guide and take on the San Juan that way.

Finding a guide was not too difficult. The whole place is set up with fly shops and guiding services. It struck me as the fly-fishing equivalent of Disneyland. The chore at hand was to try to pick the right guide. I don't mind fishing with guides. In fact, I've enjoyed some of my best fishing ever with guides. Some are famous, either on a local level or far beyond that, and you know what you're getting. After that it is a lot like blind dating. It can be great but odds are most encounters will land between fair and nightmare.

In my attempts to procure a guide without advanced reservations—and reservations seem to be a good idea on the San Juan—I ended up with the seventeen-year-old son of one of the more prominent guides. His dad came by to pat the boy on the back and pulled him aside. I could overhear some of the advice. It was a touching scene. You could see and feel the pride of the father toward the son. I knew then it would be okay. Even if the kid didn't do well, it would be honest. I'm not sure if I was his first client, but I knew I was close to that. His father was well respected and apple trees seem to grow apples. We loaded up the drift boat and the kid rowed the boat to what appeared to be an appropriate spot. I asked him if I should fish the San Juan Worm I had tied on.

He frowned. "Not if you want to catch fish."

I said, "But this is the fly named for this river."

"Yeah, but it only works at the right times."

I looked at him. I wanted to be a smart ass and say, "Of course," but I didn't want to be his first smart-ass client. Instead I swung my line over to him. He tied on a small nymph and a gob of wool about 24 inches above it. The idea was to cast the line and the wool would act like a natural bobber. The major adjustment seemed to be the distance between the fly and the wool. I looked at the proximate boats and it was indeed the method of choice, judging from what other anglers were casting. You would sit and stare at the gob of wool. It was the same stare I mastered as a young fisherman using a bobber—at times trying to channel my will into the lure, like when I was eight. Occasionally there would be a take and I would set the hook. The fish was usually a good one with a stout heart and gave a satisfying fight. I was not satisfied. In reality, this is the kind of fishing I abhor.

I turned to the kid and said, "There has to be more to this river than doing this. This simply cannot be the whole experience. All I have read ... there has to be more."

He explained that, sometimes, they do drift down the river. At this time of year, all the action was up here near the dam. I told him I wanted to drift the river. I offered him an extra hundred dollars a day. That seemed to make his eyes light up. I later found out that it was about earning more than his dad. We raise our sons that way. My dad would always ask if I was ready for a shot at the title. It is a coming-of-age thing. This time it worked in my favor. I did have to promise that if the fishing was awful I would be okay with it. Of course. Sometimes, how I fish is as important as if I catch any fish. If the act of fishing was *solely* about catching fish, I would have stopped a long time ago. The kid—that's what I called him; I forgot his name soon after the introduction—rowed the boat back to the landing and we agreed to meet after lunch. In the meantime, he would get the vehicles in place (so we could drive out from downstream) and meet me back at the landing. I was getting happier.

Lunch was good. The nice thing about fishing towns is that comfort food is always steps away. I had an open-faced sandwich with mashed potatoes and gravy to keep me satiated for the long session of afternoon fishing. I arrived at the landing and saw that the kid had a different boat. This one looked a bit newer. I said, "Nice boat, kid," and he smiled. It was his new one and he didn't want to fish it in the crowded environment by the dam. Again, you could feel the pride and desire. I love that. I have tried to keep that up over the years. It is so much easier for young people. I like being around that feeling, hoping to be infected by it.

We loaded up the boat. It was different than the way it happened in the morning. This had the feeling of promise to it. Even if the fishing was poor, I would be able to feel the San Juan underneath.

In my life I have learned that each body of water has its own distinct feel. Water is the spring from which all life came. In that truth is amazing power. Each body develops over the time it lives. The San Juan has lived a long time and was a fully endowed woman. Each body of water is like that. We explore and feel them and stay with the ones with which we fall in love. Down deep that is what I wanted from the San Juan, to feel her life.

As the boat pushed back from the landing I felt a certain exhilaration. It was but a few moments before the crowd faded and the sun felt warm on my face. I turned to the kid and asked him what fly I should try. He shrugged his shoulders and told me to try an Adams. I somehow knew he would say that or a Coachman or some other standard searching pattern. I tied on the Adams. I also had Royal Wulffs and a few other standards. It seemed that it was going to be hard. I was prepared for that. It didn't matter; the river was gorgeous. All the flora and fauna was showing itself in abundance. There were no other boats, just us. As my mind was enjoying the realization of the successful escape from the combat-fishing situation, I was also scouring my fly bag.

One of the curses of being the world's worst fly tier is realizing you don't have the power to create. A good tier has the power to artfully create and mimic the natural flow. A great tier nails it. A bad tier can only hope to acquire the magic. To that end I buy flies, lots of them. Hoping that I can pull from my bag what I need, really I'm a fraud—like the Wizard of Oz.

On that day, I stared into my bag hoping I had an answer, like giving a heart to the tin man. I kept staring, as I do, hoping something catches my eye. I pulled out an orange and white fly. Where I got it, I had long forgot; what it was called was gone too. I had a good feeling about it and tied it on. I showed it to the kid who smirked and shrugged his shoulders as if to say "why not." That first cast landed up near the far bank and was mugged, immediately. The next five casts landed fish as well. The kid asked to see the fly.

"What the hell is it?" he asked as he turned it over and over.

"I don't know," I honestly said. "I bought it a long time ago."

"Is it a dry fly?"

"It is today," I said as I swung the line and fly back to my hand and doped it up with floatant. The kid shrugged his shoulders again. As the day wore on, the fly just got hotter and hotter.

No words were spoken. It was just so good. He kept the boat in position, my casts hit the marks, and the fish ate the fly. It worked the way it was supposed to.

When we pulled out and were riding back to the landing, I asked the kid if he noticed that the further we got downstream, the more brown trout we encountered. He did notice and we decided that the next day we would fish even farther downstream.

I fished the next two days with the kid. Each day had a different feel but each day we caught fish beyond counts. It was the same process. You start to count until it gets a bit hectic and then you realize it doesn't matter anymore. Then you just get into the rhythm of the place. I felt her, the San Juan. I understood the hype. I was lucky enough to adventure away from the crowds and take a chance. I seem to be a counterpuncher, especially if it gets me off the beaten path. This is a story of counterpunches. Getting away from the storm, drifting downriver against convention, using a nameless fly, and wandering to the San Juan in the first place. It doesn't always work out but who would write about that? So we share the good times. We string them together like pearls on a necklace. Over the span of time, the moments begin to define who we are. In those three days, I did nothing but fish the San Juan. Some thinking time like that is idle and indulgent. It is my gentle sin.

Over the years, I have wanted to go back. It is a long way and time and circumstance have not permitted it. I have saved several of the flies, away from the rest, for the day I go back. I don't know if that fly will work. When I go, it will be the first fly I use. I figure, by that time it should have a name.

Somewhere, the guy who tied the pattern calls it something. That name is long lost. I have showed the fly to guys who might know. I showed it to Carl Coleman, a long time flyfisherman, guide, fly tier, writer, and expert on fly fishing the Great Lakes tributaries, and he calls it a kind of Stimulator. I sent one to my editor friend and established flyfisherman, writer, and one-time editor of *Fly Rod & Reel* magazine, and he called it an egg pattern. In truth, it is neither or both. What difference does it make?

In the end, I placed the flies in a small fly box and with an indelible marker wrote on that box—The San Juan Special. Of course.

Nonesuch Stream

It has long been an axiom of mine that
the little things are infinitely the most
important.

—*Sir Arthur Conan Doyle*

I t takes the acquisition of wisdom to understand that a happy life
is actually a mosaic of small and insignificant events. Moments like
a butterfly landing on your visor or a small hatch so localized you
imagine it was created just for you. It takes a while to get past the
ego's notions of youth. Though some people do get discovered
at the shopping mall or win millions in a lottery, big fortuitous
events are rare and in themselves cannot make happiness. For
the rest of us, we string together moments in life—like pearls
becoming a beautiful necklace.

Flyfishermen can trade in pearl necklaces for functional lan-
yards. The beads are often made up of the little things we find as
we meander without consequence to our fishing places. Any fly
fisher worth his rods has a repertoire of spots. Some are broad and
large and have so much to offer they belong to many. In a very
real way, they hold and keep fishermen. To say that the Madison
or the Frying Pan or, in my part of the world, the Beaver Kill is

one of your rivers is crazy. In those places, legends like Lee Wulff or Theodore Gordon or Rube Cross spent so much time there they merged with the environment to create a landscape. That is a wonderful and soulful thing. I hope one day I may achieve that. People might say, "Oh yes, that is the stretch Hamza would fish." That would be something.

There are places, little insignificant places, on our list that are personal and special. Often we possess them because they are overlooked by others. These places have a melody that speaks to our soul and gives us little moments that are special in a private and selfish way. Contemplating the places on my list, they are almost all accidental, incidental discoveries. Every time I encounter water my mind asks, "Is there something there for me?" In my travels I encounter water that speaks to me, repeatedly.

Years ago, I drove over a small, fast-flowing creek that was so enticing I looked for it on a Gazetteer. Directly up the mountain was a small lake. The lake was nestled in a gated private estate. Rumors over the years said that big rainbow trout were stocked into the tightly controlled lake and they persisted from year to year. I thought that it could be possible a trout or two would wash down during high-water events. Slipping over the guardrail exposed a small pool. It was no more than twenty feet across. It was impossible to fish upstream as the creek tumbled down steep, narrow, and overgrown. Downstream was just as hard. This spot was the only real fishing access. It took minutes to hook and land the first fish. My mouth fell open as I released a wild iridescent brook trout. The tiny water ran cold and hard and this managed to hold a small remnant population of Catskill brookies. Over several years, it always lightened my heart as I caught several trout, six to ten inches. I never shared it. How could I? One person in one afternoon could destroy this fragile flower. In the end, life and work took me away from this tiny slice of heaven. I did what I have not done before or since. I gave the spot to my good fishing friend, Dave. I took him to the spot and showed it to him.

"How long you been fishing this?" Dave asked.

"About five years now," I said, looking at my shoes. I could feel the burn of his stare. It was weird for a bit. I felt like I confessed to cheating at cards or teasing a baby.

"You son of a bitch," Dave said. Then something awoke in me. I remembered a time the previous fall where I felt dampness on his fly line. I asked if he was out and with the face of a guilty child, he said "no." So I snapped out of the hurt lover role and quipped back, "Look me straight in the eye and tell me you don't have any solo spots. You're a bastard for giving me shit." We looked at each other and after a pregnant paused began to laugh. I am sure Dave took the location of that place to his grave. God, I miss my friend.

Another bead on my lanyard is a quirky little river in northern Ontario. It meanders out of heavy woods with big bad mosquitos into a boggy open field. With a slight breeze to blow the bugs away, it is a pleasure to fish. I found the place on a day I was free-wheeling it. I had met this girl very far away from my home. She worked in a small restaurant by Canadian Highway 17. Her family owned what was effectively a rural northern truck stop. I had the best banana cream pie I ever ate and the loveliest strawberry blond I ever loved. If I could hit this river either coming or going I would stop there. If I was going I would have a delicious lunch consisting of a meatloaf sandwich and a hefty slice of banana cream pie.

This river had the slightest tinge of tannin. It did turn out that she was filled with northern pike all between five and nine pounds. The weird and wonderful thing about these pike is that they loved to take the worst fly ever tied. I still have a couple. They were given to me by an old relative who knew I liked to fish but had no idea about any of it. The fly is about three and a half inches long. Anything smaller than a six-weight rod will not get it in the air. It has lime green glass eyes with a black center. Its head is the size of a nickel and as thick as five nickels. The top half is a vibrant blue deer hair and the bottom half is Day-Glo orange deer hair. It has a lemon-yellow stripe going down the middle. Two black stripes band the head. Thick strands of Flashabou and tinsel are in the tail. Two green barred hackles and two orange hackles and finally dyed wool strand in green, blue, orange, and pink complete the fly.

Aside from the fact that these pike creamed a fly that resembled nothing that ever lived here, the fish looked strange themselves. They were totally lacking any markings. They were a solid silver-blue color. It was like I was stuck in a Kafka landscape. I have to admit I rather liked it.

Going north to Canada for a pretty girl, blue-silver pike, and outrageous banana cream pie was a fairly romantic notion for a young man. In spite of a warm and youthful outlook, reality set in. Some tell us that love will conquer all. It has its power but it is never absolute. It was a sixteen-hour drive, her mother (the maker of the pies) was sure I was going to end up some kind of fishing bum (who knew?) and didn't like me, and the cutest red-head you have ever seen returned my balloon to earth.

Sometimes I think we go places and love people for the purpose of finding and carrying the rarest and most beautiful pieces of glass we need for our mosaic. It seems that along with the places we hold in our hearts, people and precious commodities come too. Those spots are far from me, now, both in distance and realms. There is another spot on my lanyard that has been a bit more enduring. I call it *Nonesuch Creek*. It is a name that I took from a river in Maine. I always imagined it was to throw someone off of some kind of trail. Like those subterfuge places in Iceland and

Greenland. In my case, it is a polite way of saying, "Yeah, I went fishing but I won't tell you where."

I found Nonesuch Creek many years ago. I lived in a small apartment complex that nestled up to it. In fact, I could hear the water through the window while I lay in bed. Of course, living next to a creek, there was no chance I was *not* going to fish her. Quickly I did find out why I never saw anyone else there.

About three quarters of a mile downstream was the sewage-treatment plant. I decided that I would concentrate my efforts upstream. Some distance upstream I found a waterfall. When I stood up against it the water came to my thighs. It must have been for some mill long ago. It turned out the stream was full of little smallmouth bass. There was not a fish bigger than ten inches. This was true for the whole stream except for under the waterfall, where I catch three-pound bass at that spot.

I still go there often. It is a couple of towns over from where I live. It has become a very wealthy bedroom community for my city. They really don't seem like the kind of people who would lower themselves to fish this creek for smallmouth bass. I cannot tell you how good that makes me feel. I do love this place. I think it loves me back. I am always finding or seeing little things that bring me a smile. The bass there always do too. The last time I was there, I noticed a shiny blue glint. I walked toward it and saw it was a dark blue something buried in the mud next to my creek. When I dug it up, it was the darkest blue glass insulator I have ever found. Glass insulators used to be found atop telegraph lines, usually along railroad tracks. Most fell victim to teenage urges with twenty-two rifles or BB guns. Some people collect them, but that does not matter. It was another shiny piece of glass for my picture, for my mosaic.

I have always stated that it is the little things, in concert, that make up a good life. People that come and go. Loves that we collect. Places that take us away from the trivial and teach us about beauty and life. I have never been discovered (in a mall or elsewhere), nor have I ever won a lottery—but I have caught big bass on little poppers on Nonesuch Stream.

The Hatch

The Charm of fishing is that it is the
pursuit of what is elusive but attainable, as
a perpetual series of occasions for hope.
—*John Buchan*

One of the fundaments of our religion is the hatch. The definition of hatch that I am referring to is a verb that means to bring forth young from the egg. Of course, in fly fishing it refers to the last stage in the life of mayflies, caddisflies, stoneflies, and odds and ends of other aquatic insects. This is when the insects that trout eat follow secret and elusive cues from nature and emerge from their aquatic stage and burst forth into the air, enjoy crazy midair orgies, lay eggs, and crash and die upon the water. This sex-crazed rite of reproduction happens on most bodies of water over and over again, accommodating and perpetuating all the species of flies that happen to live there. When the flies coordinate the emergence from the surface film of the water in great numbers, their orgy triggers a feeding orgy as fish key in on the flies, which triggers an orgy of fishermen trying to present a reasonable facsimile of those flies with a hook hidden to catch the fish. Fly-fishing becomes orgiastic!

It is nice, every once in a while, to see how it is supposed to work. In truth, it seldom works that way. There are so many factors that affect the "hatch" that to be there with the right flies at the right time seems like a miracle. The worst thing that can happen to someone is to actually hit a hatch just right the first time trying. It is like going to Las Vegas and hitting the jackpot on your first pull of the one-armed bandit. You can easily spend the rest of your life trying to get back to that initial high.

It seems that regardless of when or where I go, that I am just a week late. "It is a little slow . . . you should have been here last week," I tell myself or someone points out to me, unhelpfully. My just missing the hatch would drive me up a tree. There was a time when I considered selling my services for good hard cash: Jerry Hamza's Trip Insurance—I would, for a lucrative fee, book the week after the week my customer booked his trip, thus ensuring they had a great trip. In researching the business venture, I had a friend book the week before me. It turns out he was a week late, too. I am not saying that lodge owners, guides, fly-shop personnel, and bank fishermen are liars—I am insisting they are. I know, big shocker, fishermen lying.

That fishermen are liars is not a new notion. Of all the kinds of lies the fishing lie is the most innocent. There are many kinds of lies that have varying degrees of sinfulness. "I did not have sexual relations with that woman . . . Miss Lewinsky," was a huge whopper. It seemed that people didn't mind the antics of Bill but they minded the lie. Then there are the lies of mercy: "Your ass doesn't look big in that dress! It is like they were made for each other." People don't mind these lies as they spare feelings. On the fibbing scale, just below these lies exist the fishing lies. Fishing lies also have their degrees. "Where did you catch that big lake trout?" one asks. "Oh, him? Yeah I caught him in Lake Okeechobee last August." Of all the fishing lies, "You should have been here last week" is the most innocent. "Last week" clearly being a metaphor for the last hatch. You have to be in the game long enough to understand it. That thought made me try to remember the last hatch I caught. By caught I mean hit it dead on just right.

Consider late spring last year on the West Branch of the Ausable River near Lake Placid in New York's Adirondack Mountains. By the calendar, it was late spring; by the moods of the seasons of Earth, I really could not tell. It was a very late spring, perhaps the latest of my own recollection. I was there trying to catch the legendary Green Drake hatch. As far as hatches go, it is the Green Drake that makes me crazy. I share this passion with more than a few flyfishermen. There are a few guys who bypass the Green Drakes and pray over the giant stonefly hatches, poor souls. When I first arrived, I was told, "You should have been here last week!" I grimaced and kept listening. "It was a Hendrickson hatch. My word, it was so thick you couldn't see." I felt a little better because it wasn't the Drakes hatching. Also, thick hatches can be a bit dubious. In some people's eyes, the plague of locusts in ancient Egypt was the ultimate hatch. Hatches that are too heavy make it far too hard for a trout to find *your* fly. The day I started fishing in the Adirondacks there was not much in the way of hatches happening. Toward the evening, a smattering of small black caddis showed up to create some pre-dusk activity. If you have fished the Ausable, you know that some pre-dusk browns are a very fine thing.

The following morning was cold; this whole spring was annoyingly late and cold. The fog hung in the air just long enough to be replaced by a slow, cold drizzle. Of course, this was good hatch weather. I knew in my heart it would still be too cold in general for the Drakes. But in fly fishing, you never know. It is that uncertainty that creates "a series of occasions for hope." I guess you could call me a serial hoper. I think it is this ability to look for and expect something good just around the corner that allows me to spend my life doing this. My hope was rewarded.

The reward was not the Green Drake hatch that I wanted, but a very promising Hendrickson hatch. The Hendrickson is really the white bread of fly-fishing. We look for the exotic but in our souls say grace for the staples. I fished it with some mild success but knew I needed to get the local version of the fly before the evening hatch.

I had plucked a fly off the water. I guess some call them stillborn. I took it to gauge the size more precisely. It was a size twelve. In my mind, before I took a specimen, I was guessing fourteen. There are just a couple fly shops in the area and I stumbled into the first and slapped the dun on the counter and said, "I need a bunch of these!"

The proprietor smiled and said, "Ah, the big Hendrickson's are starting. I have only got in a few of our special new imitations. They are really doing good so far."

I suddenly had the wheels in my head turning. "I will take all you have in size ten, twelve, and fourteen!"

"You want them all?" He asked with a stunned look on his face. "There must be two hundred of them."

"Yeah, give them all to me. I can't tie worth a damn. Plus, my casting stinks. Probably put fifty of them in a tree before tomorrow." I fibbed. I was trying to reduce the competition. I know, not very nice, but I did the very same thing with the other fly shop in town. I will never be a mogul of high finance. This wicked smug feeling I got from cornering the fly market must be the high those wizards on Wall Street get when they nail a market. It does come with some guilt, but I knew that at that very moment there were a couple of guys tying their asses off. For a brief moment, I fueled a fly boom in the local economy.

That evening the hatch came off beautifully. The new flies worked as good as I could have asked. The trout fought hard. It wasn't the Green Drake hatch, but it was a good solid hatch and I was in the middle of it and had two more days to fish before I had to leave. On the last morning, an older gentleman approached me streamside.

"I noticed you did very well yesterday," he said.

"Yeah, it was one of those days. It's good to see the West Branch in such fine shape. After a hard winter you just never know."

"I did fair," he said and sighed. "It seems some asshole bought all the flies that match this hatch, even bought all the sizes. I really would like to find that dick."

"*Hmm*," I hummed. "How would you like to become an asshole?"

"Come again?" he said.

"Well, the asshole who purchased all those flies is me. I have to go home after the evening hatch and I am willing to sell you most of my inventory."

He looked at me as he got redder. He tried to speak but his tongue was tied. Eventually his mouth opened. "How much?"

He was able to see the beauty in the plan. I sold him most of the flies—keeping a couple dozen for my collection. He was now the new asshole of the West Branch of the Ausable. I enjoyed the evening hatch and went home.

After recalling the last hatch I hit, I started thinking about "the one." The hatch that really hooked me. I was already pretty tied into fly-fishing (sorry, awful pun). I had fished numerous hatches. Hanging out with older, more experienced flyfishermen, I was always listening slack-jawed to their stories about the Green Drake hatches. The way some people talk about them gave an impression of being a common occurrence. They are not common. To be more correct, being at the right place and time to fish them can be frustrating. I finally decided to get to as sure a thing as there is in fly fishing.

There is a smattering of lodges located in Labrador, Canada, that have as predictable a Green Drake hatch as I have ever heard of. The tradeoff is that these places are a bit pricey. Some are so steeped in the aristocracy of fly-fishing that the "atmosphere" can be crushing. I appreciate the history of our sport—in fact, quite a bit. On the other hand, I loathe the snobbery that has evolved. In the end, I picked the one lodge I thought was good with the former and tolerable with the latter.

The side story about this quest is that it allowed me the chance to complete another life goal at the same time: Early on, I decided that a benchmark for my life in fly-fishing was that I needed to catch a five-pound-plus brook trout on a bamboo rod. I understood that this would not get me into the pantheon of the greats, but it might have me hanging coats in their lobby. My time in Labrador was wonderful. I had finally come across a solid Green Drake hatch. More than just the hatch was the way it came to happen. These bugs were big. At times size twos seemed small. They would come off here and there and the big fish cruised in slow, methodical lines, slurping down juicy morsel after morsel. You would watch a fish working and then try to anticipate its next position and cast to that spot. Then it happened. On the evening of July 20, 2004, with a nicely placed Green Drake fly, I slid the net under a 5.125 pound brook trout. It was that precise moment that I realized I was *persona non grata* as far as the human race went. I was a scratch. I was determined to fritter away all the time I could scrape together and fish. Of course, the reality is all of this sport costs money. I would have to work to fish.

One of the things I do in the coldest months is try to plan some trips for when the snow goes. At the age of fifty-one, planning to goof off makes more sense than freestyling. I do miss the freestyle. I was really good at it. I still preserve parts of that lifestyle. I will still leave without warning—the definition of a freestyle is to leave without warning—but I will find a vermin-free bed to lay my head. For the most part, I do try to plan out a trip. If I can target four or five Drake hatches a season, then I am happy. I also plan out other trips, including some hunting. I have really fallen in love with the bow. A stick and string are wonderful things.

I was visiting my mother when a fishing lodge returned my inquiry call. Those calls can just drift. If I can't be fishing, talking about it is the next best thing. She did mention that I was supposed to be visiting her. I told her it was about a trip I was thinking about. She made mention that it might be nice if I spread out my interests.

"I just can't," I told her.

"Why not? There are so many things out there," she pressed.

"I just can't. It's about that fucking thorium situation."

"I hate that word!" she shouted.

"Thorium?" I was parrying back. I always try to avoid conversations like this. I explained "that the world turned its back on thorium as a fuel for nuclear power during the sixties. That it was superior to uranium in every way except that you couldn't make it explode. The United States just couldn't get its head around anything that didn't go boom."

She was leaning back in her chair because she knew this wasn't going to end until my rant was over. I finished with the fact that if we had taken the thorium path, the meltdowns at Three Mile Island, Chernobyl, and Fukushima would have never occurred. Gas would be twenty-five cents a gallon and everyone's utility bills would be under twenty dollars a month. The world would be so wonderful except that bastard Admiral Hyman G. Rickover had to have things that went boom.

She was clearly sorry she asked, which was what I was after. I really don't give a damn about thorium. Everything I said was pretty much true but I stopped being political a long time ago. I try to do some things on a personal level. If I have extra money, I donate to a homeless shelter, or to clean up a stream I might fish. Mostly I just try (as John Gierach would write) to be the best trout bum I can be. I will arrange my trips and hope to catch a hatch or two. If I should have been there last week—well, that would be okay too.

Solstice Solace

Life is what happens to you while you're
busy making other plans.

—*John Lennon*

We try to go through this life with a master plan. Often the universe derails our master plan in such a way that we can assume that the universe's master plan resents any other. In my youth, I had an angry rebellious streak. More than trying to think outside of the box—I wanted to smash the box altogether. I wore my hair long, listened to the Haight-Ashbury tunes, and generally mistrusted the establishment. I was a non-conformist like all my friends. In those deep-thinking days, John Lennon was putting out a vibe I tried to hear. I used his song "Imagine" as my senior quote—again, with many others. Life and the rat race have a way of pounding rebellion out of most of us. In my own heart, a flicker of the flame of rebellion still burns.

If you read historians, the winter solstice has had a lot of importance. It signifies the return of the sun. Most agree that if you use the census that took place at about the time of the birth of Jesus, his actual birth was in the spring. Most likely in April. Early Christians decided to celebrate the birth of their savior during the celebration of the solstice in order to blend in. It may not have been accurate but was way better than getting eaten by lions.

So here I am roughly two millennia later and for whatever reasons the birth of a Jewish Buddhist (Ju-Bu?) who preached love and selflessness, great ideals regardless of your belief system, had been transformed by capitalistic men with no belief system into a commercial nightmare. I am a dad, granddad, husband, and reluctantly Santa Claus. I must admit this season left me even more bereft. When I get to the point of no return, my instincts tell me to run. When I was young there was always the circus, then there were Dead shows, and of course the stalwart: fly fishing.

In the instant when everyone finished opening the gifts Santa graciously bestowed, the celebration became an electronic social-media Christmas, and everyone retreated into their electronic corner. It was silent, and self-indulgent. In a way, everyone was cerebrally awash in endorphins. On the other hand, the old flicker of a flame flared up. In a short while I had slipped into my waders and was on my way to my local steelhead stream.

In the car on the way to the water, my radio was tuned into some AM station. I am not sure who listens to AM anymore. I was enjoying NPR the evening before. Instead of Garrison Keilor, AM radio had talking heads. They were discussing global warming. Indeed that day had smashed the record high for Christmas by almost ten degrees. It was nearly seventy out. It was the same old story. The granola cruncher was telling a tale of impending doom and the right-wing cash-counter was spouting that we just don't know. That this could be normal. That argument always slays me. With so much riding in the balance wouldn't it be prudent to err on the side of caution? As I pulled into the parking area I could feel my blood pressure pounding at the temples.

Much to my surprise, the lot had other cars. I got out and found a comfortable spot on the stream. The cold water felt good running over my waders. In tune with the season I started casting a green and red Wooly Bugger. It didn't matter if I caught fish. It just mattered that I was fishing. I had a very old Thomas & Thomas in my hand. She is a light bamboo 6-weight. I have found that most bamboo rods have a voice. Some special graphite rods do as well. This particular rod has a soft smooth voice. Casting her has a soothing tendency. I am not sure of how long I was casting there. It was long enough for the angry to leave. I eventually found the rhythm of the rod. The fly began to present well. As it will happen when rhythm and presentation sync up, a fish takes. This is the essence of the sport. The angling begins. All other distractions leave and for the moment it is you, the stream, and the fish. It is clean and pure. In the minutes that it took to bring the beautiful 23-inch steelhead to the net, I was perfect in my landscape.

I looked at her, the fish; she had the classic hen shape, and could feel the pride the universe had in her design. I released her gently and stood up straight. I looked around and noticed that light was retreating on this near Solstice day. When I was packing my gear to come fish, I noticed that buried behind some undelivered presents was my old coffee pot and the large coffee tin full of cedar scraps. I was on state land and building a fire was prohibited. I had that thought for a moment but clearly didn't care because it was just a few moments before I had the pot sitting on a small fire. There is something about fire that is entwined to our humanity. It was probably the control of it that led to community. In a few moments two of the flyfishermen I was sharing the water with were at my fire and shortly thereafter were waiting to share my fine Hawaiian Kona coffee. I struggled for the briefest time as I knew there was a fine, single-malt Scotch wrapped in reindeer motif wrapping paper. I did mention the struggle was brief and in minutes we were sharing dark and doctored coffee. Without words of confirmation I knew they came for the same thing.

None of us had planned to fish this day but we all needed it. We talked about past fish and future dreams. We drank the doctored brew slowly and eventually the cups emptied and the light slipped away. It was time to go back. As I climbed into the car, different talking heads were ranting until I hit the off button. I didn't want to hear it. For the time being I had a healing. I wanted to keep it. Instead I let my mind wander. I thought about going South to go fishing. Georgia? Not South enough. Florida? Keep going. It would have to be Patagonia. As soon as I was sure that Patagonia was South enough, I was in my driveway.

I opened the front door and settled in. The smell of the rib roast made my mouth water. It seemed everyone was still engrossed in their own thing. That was cool. The Wi-Fi in the house was humming with all the connections. In moments, everyone put their virtual realities aside and we gathered at the table for the holiday feast. There was lots of love at the holiday table. In many ways that is the important thing. My side trip to the stream allowed me to blow off some steam and to connect spiritually. Although unplanned it turned out to be a happy holiday. It was a Solstice soulace. I mean solace.

Good Old Rocky Top

The huntsman, he can't hunt the fox,
Nor so loudly blow his horn,
And the tinker he can't mend kettle nor pots,
Without a little Barleycorn
   —*John Barleycorn Must Die-English traditional.*

In the place where I live, the seasons come in succession with their basic identities known according to the calendar, but the accompanying mood is always surprising. Winter in Central New York is a big season and the whims of nature are many. Man, in his arrogance, is caught unawares when nature exerts her dominant will. Strenuous winters can take the form of a bad opera and be one act too long. This past winter was not a good one. Enough subfreezing temperatures and daily inches of snow can repress one's psyche. As I write this, a glance at the calendar tells me the crocuses' first brave stance against winter will still be weeks away. Perhaps months.

The captivity is self-imposed. I choose to live here. In any other season, I am proud of that choice. Here and now, I just want to get out. Once you have been driven far enough up the wall, the decision to bolt is just a given.

In my mind—the same as in yours, I'm sure—the Rolodex of organized thoughts turns slowly to options of escape. The problem is that trout need cold water. Warm places tend to be void of trout. I know there are many species that will dine on a fly. I love almost all of them. The thought of saltwater fishing in the Gulf has it sirens. But like a craving for a certain kind of sweet, my lust can, at this time of year, be satiated only by trout. I think in part I need to feel the gentle and discerning take, when a trout eats my fly. A reassurance that I am a guy who can still manage my sport of choice. Or maybe that's one of the crazy ramblings of an outdoor soul all hemmed in?

As I searched the Rolodex of options in my head, I remembered that I wanted to visit the man who had recently made me some fine fly rods. We had spent hours on the phone talking about bamboo fly rods that I wanted him to make for me. To have a craftsman who can understand what you want and be able to transcribe all the emotions and feelings that you emote to him through a piece of bamboo is something rare in life, and in fly fishing. Jim is that guy for me, a muse of sorts. Had Jim lived outside the gates of Yellowstone Park, I would have never been able to get near his rods. It was my good fortune that Jim lives in the Great Smoky Mountains. Perhaps it was a good time to visit him. It would be cold, somewhere in the forties, but warm enough. Perhaps even to fish. I had never met Jim in person but knew he would welcome a visit.

In the days after I had that thought, I called Jim and told him my plan. I asked him to recommend, if he could, a guide I might employ to fish. Jim told me to give him a couple of days and call him back. I agreed and in my mind, I knew I needed a few days to formulate a plan for the trip.

Even when we say we're flying by the seat of our pants, all trips need planning and purpose, even if that purpose is to attempt *freestyling*. You won't get very far on a freestyle trip without a budget. At this point, I'm getting a bit old for freestyling.

I do have at least one last great freestyle in me. I want to take a summer and trailer my Grand Lake Stream canoe from New Brunswick to the Northwest Territories. A half-dozen good rods, a couple of boxes of flies, and an old Rand McNally road atlas. No GPS, regardless of how sexy a British accent the machine may employ. I want to unfetter myself from technology and humanity for a whole summer. Driving across the continent and fishing where it looks good. I want no advice or pointers, I just want to go fish.

This trip to the Smoky Mountains will be nothing like that. This trip is solely to escape cold repression.

I tend to moan about the stifling qualities of modern technology but, giving the Devil his due, the internet is a good tool for getting away. I was able to find some beautiful cabins located in isolation up on a rocky top. Past beautiful, they were also affordable. Travel plans came together quickly. One of the biggest treacheries of the internet is the ease with which I become distracted. Useless bits of trivia fascinate me, and if they are history-related, then hours can drift away; the ultimate time toilet. The only saving grace would be a special edition of historical Trivial Pursuit. Actually, it's a horrifying thought to have four other people afflicted like me around a table answering questions such as a French kiss in the English-speaking world is the same as an English Kiss in the French-speaking world. It is at this point that it is best to hold one's tongue.

In the digging through the internet about this trip, I did stumble across a reference to the "southern strain of Appalachian Brook trout." I am a lover of brook trout. They are special. It was recently (in 2005) given the title as the official trout of North Carolina. Upon further searching, the many admirers of this little trout are seeking status for it as a subspecies of *Salvelinus fontinalis*. The rationale sites their diminutive size and more noticeably their spectacular coloration. The photos were beautiful and my self-expertizing persona wanted to catch one. I have gone great distances to chase these pretty fish. The thought of a little different brookie fueled my imagination.

Presently, only two sub-species are accepted for the Eastern brook trout. The first is the silver trout, which inhabited the Dublin Pond area of New Hampshire. Victimized by the usual crimes committed by man against nature, the silver trout was last seen in 1930. Inversely, the Aurora trout, native to two small lakes in the Temagami district in Ontario, Canada, has been the subject of an ecological success story. The Aurora trout is a naked brookie. It sports no spots. Thanks to good stewardship, it is now possible to catch one legally—which is on my brook-trout list. The possibility that the southern strain of the Appalachian brook trout could make this short list made me want to catch one all the more.

After making all the arrangements, I called Jim. I gave him my itinerary and the days I wanted to fish. Could he come along? Could we catch an actual wild southern Appalachian brook trout? The answers were yes and maybe and the guide I needed to call was a man named Roger Lowe because the Smoky Mountains and the trout are entwined with his DNA. I called Roger and we chatted for a bit. I could tell he was genuine and local. The best qualities a guide could have. I hired him right off.

Often we find that localities and regions transcend boundaries. They spill over arbitrary lines, which makes them harder to define. The Smoky Mountains are like that. They spill over to both western North Carolina and eastern Tennessee. The Cherokee long called the Shaconagay home. The word translates "Land of the blue smoke." The blue "smoke" sets up almost daily and is created by the respiration of the trees, which grow densely in the moist habitat. The blue tint comes from hydrocarbon emissions from the trees themselves. It makes for an eerily beautiful backdrop, and had to be a big part to the color of the local culture.

When I arrived at the cabin to set up, you could feel it. The place had history and emotion. You could feel all the cosmic energy from the mountains and it was all around. There are places I have been, most recently out West, that have been sanitized to the point where no vibe exists. That kind of shit breaks my heart. This place was just the opposite. I was excited to be immersed into the local color and to come away with an experience with fly fishing at its core.

The weather, it seemed, was going to be best the following day. Jim would not be able to make it then but he would fish with us the following day. It was decided we would float the Tuckasegee River from just above its delayed harvest point on down. The river is supposed to have great carrying capacity of native fish and also gets some heavy stocking. At this point, most of the fish have been there a while and, with hope, began the rogue process of becoming wild.

I was to meet Roger Lowe at the local Huddle House the following morning. Huddle Houses are a southern breakfast greasy-spoon chain. Actually, they are a bit more than that. They have a certain standing in southern culture. In their day, bleary-eyed truckers, drunkards, travelers, and night owls would belly up to the long counters for harsh coffee and delicious artery-hardening egg fare. Often the smoke was thick and oppressive while the 45-jukebox played Loretta Lynn. They have changed little. Of course, the smoke is gone and so are the jukeboxes, except in a few holdouts. I liked the fact I was meeting Roger at one. I would try to arrive a bit early.

Fishing with a new guide is always a bit of a dance. There are enough bad clients out there that any guide who has been at it a while is a bit cagey. They prefer to keep a professional distance. It helps if you can get past that wall. Sometimes it is very much like waltzing with a porcupine. You can introduce some grounding to help break the ice. It turns out that Roger had put out a beautiful spiral bound pamphlet called "Smoky Mountain Fly Patterns." It covered "Dry fly and nymph patterns suggested for each month and the best times to fish them, also Primary fly hatches for each month." Then there was *Roger Lowe's Fly Pattern Guide to the Smoky Mountains* with 101 traditional patterns by Roger Lowe. The guy is a master fly tier! His Sulpher pattern is a masterpiece. I knew a guy this authentic would eventually get to just plain old fishing.

When I met Roger that morning, he smiled and stuck out his paw. He was weathered but in a good way. His face belied his age by at least ten years to the good. He was fit and everything pointed to a man who made his living being outside guiding.

I rigged up a Sage 6-weight that was 8½ feet long. Roger got busy readying his pontoon raft for the day's fishing. When we were finally in the boat, Roger insisted on putting a large strike indicator on my line. It was a round float that was, in effect, a bobber. I wasn't crazy with the notion of it being there but I did understand why it was needed. The bobber was there to simply protect Roger and ensure our success. It said in bold tones that he was a very good guide and I was going to catch fish in spite of myself. Past experience has taught me to go with the flow and let my instincts guide the day.

Roger, in the beginning, had few words and stuck to the southern code of being a polite gentleman. This—coupled with his use of the indicator—told the tale of past clients. Obviously challenging people. I smiled and engaged him about our mutual friend Jim and the nice publications of Jim's that I had come across. Soon, Roger was engaged with the oars and I was laying down my first cast.

Cold is relative, with lots of modifiers. The morning was about 40 degrees. The sun was out and shining bright. The radiation from the hydrogen fusion was on my face and it felt nice. The same rays were penetrating the water and slightly and slowly adding warmth. The question in situations like this is, "Will it be enough to matter?" That question was quickly answered with my hookset on a pretty rainbow trout. She was all of nine inches sporting that beautiful pink slash down her sides. It was easy to tell she was a wild fish. I was glad of that, too. I had come a long way to find this moment. It was something just to hook up, but her being wild was good medicine. I hooked and landed several more fish. There's nothing like catching fish to lubricate a situation.

At about this time, I took off the strike indicator. I assured Roger that I might miss a fish now and then, but I would not miss all of them. Right then, I missed a fish and cursed in a way that caused Roger to smile and repeat the curse as a question. It's not often you can delineate the moment you create a friendship—but at that precise moment, Roger and I realized enough common ground for one.

I had lots of questions for him. The problem was, I kept getting interrupted by fish. At first you start counting fish. Why? I guess we try to qualify life with verifiable quantities. It was still very early when we had landed a dozen trout. It was at that time we noticed that the fishing was good and that we needed to really start paying attention and have one of those big days.

Clearly, Roger was a great guide. He knew where the fish were—and more importantly, he understood boat control and where to hold the boat for his left-handed client. When a trip is going as it is supposed to, the guide, boat, and client all fall into an efficient rhythm.

We kept catching fish—mostly rainbows, with a few brook trout mixed in. The brookies were stocked fish and not southern Appalachian strain brook trout. In other words, they were the same fish I chase everywhere, wherever brook trout are found— they were not the fish I had been hoping to find here in the Smoky Mountains. I wanted to catch and hold and see with my own eyes one of those Appalachian-strain trout. I wanted to feel them with my own soul, to see if they were . . . different. These were not Appalachian trout. They were the Eastern brook trout

I was intimately familiar with, the fish of my heart's infatuation, and that was just fine.

Eventually, I got to the point where I stopped counting. In a spiritual way the oppression that caused me to find this place was lifting. I was past the need to qualify it. With humans all things are spiritual; it is spirituality that drives our sentience. The real question is the quality of it all and this was just getting better and better.

Roger's flies were beautiful and flawless. I am always in awe of master fly tiers. Over and over, I have tried to improve my fly tying but my flies always end up looking like I pulled a wad of gum from under the couch. Because of my deficiency, I buy lots of flies. To that end, I had with me a box of bead heads with metallic flash tied to the fly. At some point, I always feel the need to tie on a fly from my fishing bag. I guess it is just a client's way of saying, "I have done this before." I pulled out a size 14 silver bead head fly with a silver tinsel body. I asked Roger how he liked it. He smiled and said, "It's very, very bright, isn't it? You never know, it might work." It did work. I'd had some success with steelhead on those flies. Every time the fly brought a fish to the net, Roger smiled. He eventually and affectionately started calling it the "silver bullet."

The day went on—and as all good days do, it finally started to wane. I was not sure how many fish we caught but I did know it was past fifty. It was the last day of January and I had a fifty-plus fish day in the Great Smoky Mountains. A fifty-plus fish day is a feat, anytime. In the dead of winter, it is pure delight. Stealing a halcyon day off the heap.

We decided to meet the following morning at the Huddle House; this time Jim would be with us. The plan was to get into the nearby national park and fish a small stream at a higher elevation. If I wanted to catch an honest-to-goodness southern-strain Appalachian brook trout, this is where we needed to be.

Fortunes had turned, as far as the weather went. It was ten degrees colder than the day before and dark low clouds in the distance were coming our way. Roger, Jim, and I took to Roger's vehicle to make the drive. It was a lengthy but pleasant ride. We talked about the area and we talked about all the fishing in and around the Great Smoky Mountain National Park. The people were descendants of non-English, English subjects. They left the highlands of the Isles and settled into similar territory in the new world. Part of their reason for coming was a stubborn rebellious streak that passed down to current generations. No king would rule them and the fierce independence helped them survive the tough and stingy mountain life. From the roots in Europe, they brought with them music of the highlands and also their recipe for *uisce beatha*. (Gaelic for "water of life.") Both Roger and Jim had strong connections to this heritage. Most people in the Appalachians do.

We pulled alongside a small stream adorned in mountain Laurel. It was steep with boulder falls and plunge pools. The first glance screamed brook trout to me. Pristine small water. Lots of plunges for oxygen.

The three of us spilled out of the truck and strung up rods. As I was pulling the leader past the top eye, I noticed my fingers losing dexterity. It didn't take long for the cold to set in. You could see ice accumulating on the edges of the beautiful stream. We fished hard for a couple of hours. There were no takes, there were no flashes—there was just cold. We managed to approach the truck at the very same time. The looks on each face told the same story. It was just too cold and the ominous clouds had caught up with us. The freezing rain that was falling shut the door.

I knew the diminutive brook trout were there. They were just turned completely off. Like missing the kiss at the door on a first date, my passion burned even brighter. I knew I was coming back.

The car ride back afforded more conversation, and for me, a deeper understanding of the area. The two men had fly fished here all of their lives, and so did their fathers before them. The area has a fly-fishing culture that rivals almost anywhere.

Then the conversation turned to moonshine. Moonshine had so many names—alley bourbon, bush whiskey, catdaddy, corn liquor, corn squeezins, donkey punch, hooch, hillbilly pop, mountain dew, mule kick, pine top, popskull, red eye, rot gut, sugar whiskey, tiger's sweat, and white lightning—to name but a few. I liked the one Roger used the best. He called it white liquor and it had a respectable sound to it.

Any history of the Appalachians includes the importance of making the white liquor. The roots of the moonshine industry can be traced back to colonial days. The illegal spirits helped many an Appalachian family to survive. The white liquor was easy to make, never got any better than the moment it dripped from the copper tube, and families brewed their own recipes with pride.

Of course, being a born and bred Yankee, my exposure to the brew was mostly from television. If you watched *The Waltons*, you were familiar with the Baldwin sisters' prized recipe. The other show was *The Beverly Hillbillies*. Granny was always toting a jar with XXX marked on the side. Turns out that each "X" represents how many times it has been run through the still. Three Xs represents almost pure alcohol. The best days for the moonshiners came from prohibition. It became highly profitable, and that cast the die for many years to come. During this era, conflicts really heated up between the distillers and the law. With a need to outrun the law, guys with names like 'Ol Bad Eye, Buttermilk, Goober, or Cooter built some heavily modified engines. As the NASCAR hardcore will tell you, this was the beginning of their sport.

I asked Jim and Roger about the importance of moonshine in their families, which they both verified. In their memories, when the boys came home from WWII, there was little to no work. Being independent was so important. Public assistance was far beneath their proud heritage. Roger told a story of his great uncle.

"He was riding in his truck down along a mountain road. Up a little ways he came across an old man alongside the road. It was chilly and the old man had himself wrapped in a blanket while hitchhiking. My uncle stopped and picked up the man. In a short while, the man pulled out a jug from under the blanket and told my uncle to drink. My uncle, telling of promises made to his Christian mother, politely declined. The old man put a gun in my uncle's face. The hitchhiker ordered my uncle to drink. Well, my uncle took a pull and remembered it burning from his chin to his toes. A moment later the stranger put the pistol into my uncles hand and said, "Okay, now it's my turn, hold the gun on me." That was his uncle's beginning into the moonshine business. It was a colorful tale, one of which most families have a version.

Moonshine or white liquor has come mainstream. It has become, for all purposes, legal. You can go to any liquor store and buy it. It even has become somewhat stylish and you can buy it infused with different flavors. That leaves a certain nostalgia for previous days.

That evening, back at the cabin I paired a glass of liquor with a Nat Sherman Perlas cigar. On the deck looking down on the Smokies, the cabin had a hot tub. The air was cold but the water was 104°F. I was taking in the events of the last couple of days, and thinking about where I was.

Memory is funny. Who knows what stimulus will ignite what memory? Sitting there, in the tub, with fine drink and smoke, my memory flashed back to my youth. I was eleven or twelve, hanging out on stage before one of the country music concerts my father and grandfather had promoted. It was a Conway Twitty tour and the band was warming up. One musician had a Martin guitar across his lap. Another musician was admiring it.

"Yes, sir," he said. "It was given to me by my daddy. It's a 1939. He was a preacher in Cherokee, North Carolina."

"It has that sweet sound," the second musician said.

"Yeah, I love her. A Yankee offered me five thousand for her."

"Really? I would have busted him in the head!"

"Well . . . let's just say he was done asking."

They realized I was there and changed the conversation. The heritage underneath the conversation all those years ago finally came into focus. This was the home of bluegrass music. I had always known that the music and the old instruments (money was tight so when you got one it was special) were legendary, and that Martin guitars were passed on for generations. I liked this culture. The fact that fly fishing was such a big part of it was unknown to me, until now.

The Osborne Brothers released the song *Rocky Top* on Christmas day in 1967. If you listen to the words, it's about a longing for home in the Smokies, about longing for a simpler time.

The time I spent there was sweet. It was simple and disconnected. I spent the week with my cell phone turned off. I went fishing and visited friends. All the while the backdrop and vibe of the Great Smoky Mountains made it a good week. It made my escape complete.

The Tree of Knowledge

> You see, in this country are a number of
> youths who do not like to work, and the
> college is an excellent place for them.
> —*L. Frank Baum from Ozma of Oz*

College is a place for all kinds of learning. I freely and openly admit I spent copious amounts of time fly fishing during my college years. At commencement, I remember an advisor who figured out that I might have been the only graduate with an attendance rate of less than 5 percent. To be fair, I did read the material—but I resented classes in which material was regurgitated back to me. Oftentimes, when I went to class I'd move my lips along with the professors. Fuck that—so I went fishing. You'd think college professors really wouldn't care but, so often in life, if you think someone wouldn't care, sure enough some will. Usually, principle is called upon as the justification for caring.

The principle that came into play here was an accounting professor named Tom Sears, who had recently become cranky in part because his side business, Sears Tax Returns, was going to have to be called something else. A large department-store company named Sears—even though Tom assured them otherwise—felt that it infringed upon the name they had copyrighted. They assured Professor Sears it was not personal but really a matter of principle. So in the spirit of all the principles going around, and to solely slow down my fishing, Professor Sears instituted mandatory attendance in his class. The policy was: a half-grade would be deducted per unexcused absence. After announcing the policy, Professor Sears let my fellow classmates know they had me to thank for it. To say my popularity suffered would be an understatement. I would need to take an Accounting II course the following semester. As I went to register, a crowd of my classmates was waiting for me.

In the land of higher learning, some actually practice the learning part. (Many indulged in the higher part, as well.) They were waiting for me, not out of brotherly love, but to watch my enrollment. In that way, they could avoid Tom Sears's mandatory attendance. It took several moments for me to figure it all out but once I did I decided to have fun with it. I spent the better part of an hour oscillating between time slots. My mild amusement ended when someone shouted, "Hamza, stop being such a jerk."

The following week, I was in the front row of Professor Sears's Accounting II course with a large grin. It was a smile that had no company. The professor looked up in amazement. "Looks like it's just me and you," he said. I told him that his accounting skills were already impressive. It took about two weeks of me sitting in the front row sporting mirrored sunglasses, quite motionless, until I broke my silence.

"Don't you have any questions?" Tom Sears asked.

"No, not at all," I replied.

"Are you even paying attention?"

"At times."

"Why don't you?" he asked.

I said, "Look, I read the homework and do the worksheets. So far I am good."

At that point we agreed that this was just silly. He decided that he could use his time in a much better way. The end result was that I would take exams with the other section and call him at home if I had any problems. As it was the middle of March, I was pretty excited that I would be ready for the April 1st trout-season opener in New York State.

Later that year, I was fishing one of my favorite little streams. It was a pretty May day and I was enjoying coaxing the occasional brown trout to strike my fly. As I worked my way upstream, coming around a bend I ran smack into my biology class on a field trip. Before I could finish the thought "Oh shit!" a booming voice could be heard—"Mr. Hamza, so nice of you to make our field trip. I see you have taken the initiative of doing some surveying downstream."

I was busted. Trying to worm my way out of situations has never been my style. As a fly fisher, worming just seems wrong.

The professor was a great man. His name was Dr. Earl Deubler. He was smart and witty. I enjoyed him and thought he possessed an inordinate amount of humanity for an authoritative figure. Aside from being my teacher in this course, he was chair of the Biology Department and for his penance he was my advisor.

He walked over to the abutment of the small bridge that stretched over the stream. "Mister Hamza, can I see you please?"

I walked to him, with my head slung low and my rod angled downward in a submissive posture. The less-mature students in the class were snickering and whispering. Oddly enough, I always thought those people would outgrow that behavior. I was wrong. They still snicker and whisper; it is a natural-born characteristic of the lesser American asshole. (I guess I learned some biology after all.) As I got to the professor, he turned toward the bridge and so did I. In a low voice he asked, "How's the fishing?" I looked at him with raised eyebrows. "How's the fishing?" he asked again.

I stammered, "Um . . . it was great. . ."

We talked for several minutes. He looked at my setup. He asked if I fished this riffle or that hole. After several minutes he asked if I fished the section of the stream that went through the tiny town several miles upstream.

"No," I replied, "I figured that it is so easy to fish that it must be wiped."

"Well, for the most part it fishes slow," the professor said. "Out behind the fire hall is a massive oak tree. Its roots stretch out under the stream from one side of the bank to the other. I want you to fish it slow and be in my office at 11:00 in the morning."

I was dumbstruck. "Really?"

"Yes, and you better be there."

At this point I was confused and thought it better to do what he requested. I began trekking upstream past some slack-jawed classmates. I turned to the professor and waved and he waved back and shouted, "Good luck!"

It always amazes me when I finally figure out something remarkable that has been hiding in plain sight. I had passed by that fire hall many times. In my fishing consciousness, the section of the stream that rolled through the little town was just too . . . well, out in the open. I could not recall ever seeing a soul fishing it. I pulled into the parking lot behind the fire hall, almost next to the oak. There was no reason to try and figure out which oak. Though there were several oaks there was only one "The Oak." I took my time setting up my rod and reel. All the time I was seeing that glorious tree for the first time. It was at least forty feet high. Its circumference was perhaps ten feet. It had that classic lollipop shape with craggy dark bark. It held a massive bright green canopy as new leaves tend to vibrate with the ebb of the sap coursing through the living tree.

My mind recalled a trip to the Toronto science center a few years earlier. One of the exhibits was a massive oak tree, similar to this one. It hung from a great ceiling with its roots carefully exposed. The scientific point was to illustrate that the trees had a root system nearly identical in size to the leaf canopy. The tree at the science center was more than four hundred years old.

I looked at this oak. How old was it? The chances were very good that it split the shell of its acorn well before our founding fathers were born. (I have to stretch years against events. Just to see them written really doesn't mean much otherwise. When people start talking in cosmic units of time I just cannot wrap my brain around it.) As I slowly and quietly made my way to the fishing spot, I looked up into the tree. I knew its roots stretched the whole area its canopy covered. It covered the whole of the stream bottom and almost to the far side. I was on that far side walking on a trail. The trail was old and worn. It wasn't well worn. The difference is that it was used for a long time but not all the time. I wondered how much of the path was worn by the professor from the college?

It was one of those nice May days. Sunny but still a bit cool. A small hatch of something was coming. I was really into small hatches of small flies, then. My eyes were good. A size 18 fly was still easy to see coming off the water. That's the problem with easy—it keeps getting harder. I like small dry flies. I could set the flies upon the water with such a lilt. It was one of the first self-seductions I had enjoyed. Innocent, too. I was not really even aware of that danger. Danger? I was casting intently and with purpose all around that great tree and all its feet reaching out into the current. Much to my surprise I had managed to wrangle a couple of very respectable brown trout. As I was looking across the water, I could feel a gust of wind blow through my hair. I turned my face toward the sun. In a moment I could see an object fall from the canopy. There is something in our minds that records memorable moments hard and deep into our memory. So amazing is the human brain that I can, to this day, replay that moment in my mind's eye slowly, vividly, and clearly. The baby robin fell into the water with a *gallump*. As it bobbed to the surface, a lightning streak of brown swirled from some unseen place and opened its maw. In one gulp the bird, fish, and moment were gone. For the next hour I sat there looking at the spot. I was trying to make some sort of fly-fishing and universal order of all this.

I don't know why but I did tie on a different fly. How do you match that sort of hatch? I knew it would never work but I fished the spot for the better part of the afternoon. It went dead and cold. Enough carnage had occurred in that pool, for now. Was that fish there waiting for this feeding opportunity? That was the question that bore into me for the rest of the day and a sleepless night.

The next day, as I walked to Deubler's office, I was alternating thoughts of that brown trout and what the topic of the upcoming meeting might be. The hallway was dimly lit. You could smell the acrid and stale smell of the years of tobacco burning. I was amazed that all these great minds of scientific learning mostly had smoking in common. I knocked on the frosted glass of his wooden door. The booming voice beckoned me to come on in.

"I wasn't sure you would come," the professor said.

"I always keep my appointments," I replied.

"Unless it means going to class. You don't seem to keep many of those. You only kept yesterday's by accident," he said as he smiled.

I looked sheepishly at the ground, not knowing what to say. Much to my relief the conversation moved to fishing.

"So, did you make it to the oak?" he asked.

I told him I did, and then I took my time and told the whole fishing tale with emphasis on the baby robin. He told me that he wasn't familiar with "that" fish but he knew well of that behavior.

"Do you think he was there waiting on baby birds to fall?" I asked the dean.

"I can tell you that it is almost surely what he was doing. I have seen this sort of meat-eating super trout before." And then he asked, "What were you fishing?"

I told him the flies I used that day and they were all size 16 or smaller.

"Do you think giant trout eat small flies?" he asked. "I can assure it is only a fluke if they do. It is a matter of making a living. Simple basic biology. It takes energy to move a big body like that. If it eats things that cost it more energy than it gets in return then it's out of business."

I looked at the professor. I knew what he was getting at. I always knew it. The real problem is all those stories of giant trout taken on a size 22 fly. It romanticized the event. Giving it an almost David versus Goliath feel. We discussed how statistically significant upgrading to a bigger fly could be in the hunt for bigger fishes. Then the lesson at the fishing tree of knowledge offered a real question that lies at the heart of the sport. How do we fish and why do we choose to pursue to fish that way?

It is a big question and the answer relies on factors that are different at times. Do we fish? Do we quest for big fish? Think a bit on it.

We chatted for the better part of the afternoon. I saw that he was pleased that he made me learn. Then he learned that I loved to learn.

"Can I ask something a bit personal?" said the professor.

"Go ahead," I replied.

"All the time you are absent from class . . . are you trying to say that you are fishing during that time?"

I was uncomfortable about the question but felt I needed to lay down my cards. "I can tell you that if I am not fishing I am hunting or looking for ginseng or whatever the season dictates. I picked this college so I could be outside. My biggest fear is that when it is over—my time at college—I will be forced behind some sort of desk and that will be it."

After a pause, Dr. Deubler spoke. "You know much of the staff figured your high absenteeism was just your inability to make it to class as a result of partying. That you are spending it afield is interesting."

After that meeting, things changed. The staff started to look at me in a slightly different light. I was viewed more as a rogue than a degenerate drunk. I was encouraged to write a few articles as the "Wick Sportsman" for the school paper. My reputation was cemented as one who marched to a different drum. At the end of the semester, I received a letter from my advisor. It included a large Mickey Finn and a short note that read, "Swing for the fences." I felt like I should fish the tree by the fire hall once more before I went home for the summer.

I was casting the big colorful Mickey Finn next to the big colorful tree. The fishing was slow but the thinking was not. I was thinking of all I learned because of this tree. I learned: Big fish eat big meals; great life lessons come from trees of knowledge; and not all of them are conventional.

In this state of thinking, my casting often suffers. The streamer hung up high in a branch on the mighty oak. I pulled and, as often is the case, the leader returned without the fly. The fly adorned the tree for the remaining two years of my college career. I like to think it is there still. A connection over time. I think about the lesson there. That learning is so much more than ontogeny leads to phylogeny.

In my children, I notice a spark that is similar to mine. I think the trick is to find a way to give that spark direction. I enjoy people with the spark of life. You just never know what an oak tree will teach you while you're trying to catch pretty brown trout.

An Occurrence at the Fifteenth Hole

In the immortal words of Jean Paul Sartre:
'Au revoir, gopher.'
—*Carl Spackler in the movie* Caddyshack

Ihave been exposed to golf, minimally, so I am okay with it. I really try to stay away from golf courses, especially country clubs, as the high criminal element makes me nervous. I have to mention that O. J. Simpson was an avid golfer and so were all the American presidents of the last fifty years. I think these two bits of evidence alone make my case. If all things were equal, then I could just look the other way and go on with my life.

Unfortunately, all things are not equal. On many golf courses all over the continent you'll find water hazards ranging from puddles to honest-to-goodness lakes. Often, these bodies of water harbor populations of big fish that have never seen a fly. A thing like that can keep a guy up at night. I've tried to ignore it. Like trying to ignore an itch, it can't be done. In fact, it flares up into a major infatuation. In the end, I broke down and began sneaking onto golf courses after dark.

I had some glorious evenings in my late teens and early twenties, catching monster bass on beautiful summer nights. Some fishing, some skinny dipping, but I was not too skinny so really it was just nude swimming. For some unknown reason, the rich and privileged seemed to mind that a young guy was enjoying himself on a resource no one else ever used. Eventually things heated up. I would go from course to course, trying to keep things mixed up. The courses started to share information. Eventually I would get caught and get dragged in front of the judge. Then I would get dragged in front of another judge. In the end, I was finally told that if I appeared again, they would lock me up and throw away the key. It is only an educated guess that more lawyers play golf than fly fish.

Years later I would have a neighbor named John. He was a good sort. Our lives were running down different paths. I was traveling with George Carlin as one of his managers and John was climbing the corporate ladder. John and I would hang out together and fish, play with cars, drink, smoke, and swear, and of course barbeque. Up to that point, John was the best neighbor I ever had. Whenever things are going smoothly, I always wait for the other shoe to drop. Of course, it finally did. One afternoon while we were burning some nice steaks on the grill, John turned to me and said, "I think I am going to start playing golf." I just looked at him. "Did you hear me?" he asked. I just kept looking at him.

"What?" he said.

"You know what!" I sneered back.

"It's not really that bad," he tried to reason.

"Yes it is. You're a rat bastard!" I muttered. "I'll talk to you later. I'm going home."

I avoided John for the better part of the week. Finally, his wife cornered me and explained things. John's boss told him that he should start playing golf, that it would be good for his career.

That's how it is with big corporations. They want to tell you how to work and how to play. I was sympathetic to my friend. I went next door and told him I might be willing to help. I also informed him I was not ever going to wear any of those ridiculous clothes. That if he started to wear them I would not go with him.

John said, "You think you look any better in some of your fishing outfits?"

"You are really treading on some sacred ground," I quipped back. "If you want me to help, you'd better get a lot more sensitive, fast." I went on to ask, "What do you have in mind?"

John replied, "I was hoping you would join a country club with me?"

I began to turn red. I hated golf, I hated the white-collar criminals that would not let me fish on their courses, and I despised all the arrogance the places exuded. I turned to John. "You know I am an Italian-Lebanese Catholic and you ... you're Irish and Puerto Rican Catholic. The only fucking way we would get on any country club in this town is if we wore waiter's uniforms." He looked at the ground, a little sheepishly as he knew what I said was true. John was an indomitable sort and I knew he would be back.

While I waited for him to come at me with a plan, I began to think it over. I knew I would never golf. Somewhere deep inside me were those old stirrings of the great time I had fly fishing those course waters. In a few days, as predicted, John came over. He began telling me about this equal opportunity golf course called Lakeview. It seems that in most towns there is a course that is set up for those who are not of the "skull and bones" crowd. They really take almost anyone, the exceptions being serial killers and insurance salesmen. John's face was glowing. He was so happy—there was even a two for one discount, he told me. I broke down and agreed. He was so happy he nearly kissed me on the mouth.

The next day I started looking for golf stuff in earnest. I was diligent. I knew I didn't want to pay too much for this shit. The first thing on my list was a big tall golf bag. I found one at a garage sale that was at least four feet tall. It was a very old, very big leather bag. I was so proud. I then went to look for clubs. It seems that left-handed clubs are a bit more expensive than right-handed ones. It is also that way with some hunting and fishing equipment. I was determined to help John, and I finally ended up at a garage sale that had two rusty clubs. One was a wood of some kind and the other a seven iron. They were both right handed. I offered seventy-five cents for the pair. I couldn't wait to show John.

"Hey, look what I bought!" I shouted from his driveway. He came outside and initially smiled when he saw the bag. As he got closer his smile melted away. He didn't want to hurt my feelings.

"You know, Jerry, um," he stammered. "I don't know how long these will hold up. That bag is giant. Where did you get these?"

I was just beaming with pride. "Garage sales. I paid less than five dollars!"

"Hey man, are you short cash?"

"No, I'm fine. I figured these will work great."

"You don't even have a putter!"

"I know. I didn't want to clutter up the bag with too much golf stuff."

"That bag is huge!"

"I know, but I want to make sure I have enough room for my fly gear." I was by then smiling ear to ear.

"*What?*" John moaned.

"Did you really think I was going to play golf," I giggled. "I will support you but I am fishing all those great ponds."

John's frown was the inverse of my smile. He would be all right. I know that he knew deep down he was never going to see me tee off and say "fore." As for the ponds at Lakeview, they were something. Lakeview was on low-lying land and more than a bit swampy. It was totally unsuitable for housing so they drained the land by digging numerous big ponds and turned it into a golf course. It was truly the low end of the private golf scale, but they did accept us. I was really excited to go with John. There were rumors that the pond at the twelfth hole had bluegill as big as dinner plates.

That first season was like a slice of heaven. We had the system down: John would drop me off at one of the ponds, he would shoot three or four holes, and then take me to another. It was such a good arrangement. The twelfth hole did indeed have bluegill as big as dinner plates; it also had very large bass, jumbo perch, snapping turtles . . . (cue the tune "12 Days of Christmas") Canada geese a-shitting and a blue heron in a pine tree. I was truly in my glory and unfortunately John's game was improving to the point where he would kid around about being the "Puerto Rican Tiger Woods." I was left scratching my head.

There are many different philosophies—Axiology, Agnosticism, Bioethics, Bushido, *Cogito ergo sum*, Dualism, I could go on. I am by nature an Entropist. By the nature of entropy, a gradual decline into disorder makes it impossible to keep as a philosophy. I believe that nature abhors any philosophy trying to build anything in the face of her relentless entropy. Even if you are a Big Banger, you believe the endgame comes when all matter collapses upon itself, so you believe in some order of things. Physicists tend to make me uncomfortable. Their endless march to explain the universe as a Godless place just seems so mean spirited. What I am really trying to say is that our first season went so well that I was wondering how long it would stay so wonderful.

The answer to that little question came sooner than I would have liked. It began when John received a letter from Lakeview. It seemed that their fleet of dying old golf carts was becoming too expensive to maintain. We were given the choice to keep renting on a limited basis, thus facing the reality that there may not be one when we wanted to rent. The other choice was to buy one from them or elsewhere and keep it at the course.

One of the things John and I loved to do was work on cars. I was a decent engine guy; John was a master when it came to body repair and paint. We decided to buy one of the used carts. It was, in short, a piece of shit. I rebuilt the motor, which was a good winter project. When I was done I had parts left over, as I always did. Even with that, the motor purred. They always did; it was a Zen thing.

It was a cold and dark Saturday morning when John asked me to bring over the motor. He was tight-lipped about the job he was doing on the body. When he raised the garage door, I just stood there with eyes welling up and tongue hanging out the side of my mouth. John had done her in a lime green metal-flake, clear-coat paint. From red headlights, lemon-yellow flames went halfway back on the length of the cart. The back end sat a good six inches higher than the front. This was all capped off with beautiful chrome wheels. She was gorgeous. I mounted the engine and we decide that a muffler would only ruin the effect. We were so ahead of schedule that we modified the back end to accommodate a half keg, a cooler, and an auxiliary blender. Finally, at my insistence, we gave her a name painted on the back, "The Fishin' Mission." We were ready for the season.

That second season was a good one, as well, though we started drawing attention to ourselves. We started to employ walkie-talkies. Mobile communication helped both our games. We were loud but we were having fun. Most of our fellow golf-ers liked our partnership. Most days, by the time we got to the eighteenth hole, darkness would be falling. I was even getting philosophical. I often would just watch the water without fishing to contemplate each pond and to see if that would show me their subtle selves. I took fishing there in a very spiritual way. One evening at the pond at the fifteenth hole I was watching the beginning of a feeding frenzy. It was warm and peaceful with a cool breeze. I was watching with a keen eye. At that moment, an older woman golfer came up to me.

"Hi!" she said. I jumped, clearly startled. I was so deep in concentration I didn't notice her approaching.

"Hi," I replied with a smile.

"You looked so lost, just staring at the water." Her concern was evident.

Not wanting to reveal myself, I said, "Well, you see, I lost my last ball in the water hazard. I am trying to decide if I should go in and get it or just quit the round here."

She told me to hang on and began to walk toward her cart. At that moment, an enormous largemouth bass broke the surface and took down a whole adult blackbird. My eyes were bugging out of my head. The fish had to be near ten pounds. I felt a hand on my shoulder. I was caught off guard again.

"My, aren't you a jumpy guy," she said.

I smiled. "Yeah, it's from the war." I figured what the hell. As far as lying goes I may as well make it the kind any fisherman would be proud to tell.

"Oh, you poor thing," she replied patting me on the shoulder. She stuck out her other hand and said, "Here, these are for you. I hope you finish with a nice score. Golf is supposed to calm you."

She handed me a three pack of new Titleist balls. I thanked her for her kindness and even felt a little bad about the fibs. A moment later my head riveted right back to the occurrence at the fifteenth hole. All that was left were a few black pin feathers floating on the water. I know there are places in Florida and California where a ten-pound bass is nice, but here in Upstate New York that is a legendary fish.

Eventually the Giant of the Fifteenth became an obsession. It was not long before it was the worst kept secret at Lakeview. People would ask if I had seen him again. Did I think I would get a shot at him? Was he really that big? It would be the undercurrent buzz for the rest of that season. I even began enjoying going to the clubhouse. (Good fishing can cover almost any sin.) At the same time, we converted the back of the cart to a fully stocked bar. Other people started to carry walkie-talkies and when anyone shot an eagle or better, we would turn on the red flashing light on top of the cart and rush over to the shooter. We would offer a booze shot of their choosing.

Toward the end of that second season John and I received a letter in the mail. We were both summoned to the Lakeview president's office the following Monday. It had all the feel of going to the principal's office so many years earlier. The main difference being I was now a grown man and there were limits to the amount of crap I would swallow. Monday came and John and I were walking down the dimly lit hallway to the president's office, all along the way seeing photos of Walter Hagen. He was a local boy, and everything I had read led me to believe I would have liked him, that there was a good chance he might have liked to share a glass of whisky and a fine cigar while looking into the pond for the course giant. That amiable image was dispersed the moment we opened the door to the president's office.

Replacing the genteel image of Hagen was an old man with white hair and a yellow mustache. His white eyebrows curled over the top of his wire-rimmed eyeglasses. The most noticeable feature was his hard frown, which announced, "I'm an asshole." Every once in a while, you meet someone that looks entirely contrary to their first appearance. Not this guy. He was a hundred-and-two-year-old asshole. He kept mentioning the sanctity of the game. *Wha wha wha* and the sanctity of the game. He pointed his bent arthritic finger in my general direction.

"You're the one who fishes instead of golfs! If I find so much as one can of worms . . ." By this time his face was a true magenta.

I pointed my thick finger back. "Worms?" I shouted. "You will never find worms on me!" And now my face was turning shades of red, too. John was being as diplomatic as the scene allowed. He began to hold me back (giving me the stink eye) while at the same time giving the old guy a bunch of lip service. It was then I noticed John was indeed getting good at the corporate way of doing things. He spread so much bullshit so fast that the president was mumbling under his breath about keeping an eye on me but would let it slide. At the same time, John had me laughing as we walked back down the hall. Everybody liked John. He could really let the blarney fly.

It was late that second season when the fates stepped in. I was hit by a moment of clarity. If Walter ate a large black bird, why not throw a big black fly? Everyone had, by this time, started calling the big fish "Walter." It was a reference to the big trout in the Henry Fonda and Katherine Hepburn film *On Golden Pond*—or so I thought. I was fond of both actors and I was also very fond of the Adirondacks, where the movie was set. I rather enjoyed that everyone was calling my fish Walter. And Walter agreed with my brainstorm and slurped my big, black fly. The event I had been waiting for, the event all the members at Lakeview CC had been waiting for, was on. Walter was every bit as bad natured as I hoped. I really did have my hands full. I hoped John was nearby.

John and the cart with my net were nowhere in sight. At the same time, I noticed Walter was fighting his way toward a half-submerged pine tree felled in a recent wind storm. I knew if he made it to the tree it would be over, Walter knew if he made it to the tree it would be over, and a voice from behind me blurted, "If he makes it to that tree it's gonna be over!" I turned quickly to see a regular and his partner standing beside me watching events unfold.

I asked, "Hey buddy, would you reach inside my pocket?" He looked at me sideways. I said, "Don't be a degenerate. Call John on my walkie-talkie." The spectator agreed and began shouting "Breaker-breaker, looking for John, Walter Hagen has been hooked on the fifteenth and we need the net. Come in, John!"

"Walter Hagen?" I thought. All along I was thinking about the big, stout, legendary trout character in a wonderful movie about living all the way to the end. It never occurred to me that anyone would think anything else. But it made sense. These folks were golfers and Walter Hagen was a big golf character. Sometimes you just have to accept things. Walter Hagen.

Meanwhile, golf carts began to stack up on the fifteenth like cars at the mall on Black Friday. More and more people were coming, but no John. I was getting stressed. Walter was giving me a workout, I pulled back until the leader began to sing. At the same time, various advice was being shouted at me from the peanut gallery. "Don't horse him! Keep him out of that tree, play him easy, don't hurt Walter." None of it helped. Right then all I wanted to see was John's round face with the net.

As in a good Western movie, where the calvary shows up just in time, John finally made it.

"Hey man, I'm dying here! What the hell?" I growled at him.

"I am sorry, dude," John pleaded. "I was stuck in traffic!" He gestured to all the people around us. An honest to goodness crowd was jumping around. I put all my attention and skill into fighting Walter Hagen. Finally, I got the great big bass to a place where John could slide the net under him. In a moment, Walter was hoisted out of the water. A cheer went up and people were pushing and shoving to see the fish. Someone asked what I was going to do with him. It was never in doubt: Walter would be allowed to go back to his home. He was weighed and photographed. It didn't matter that he was a smudge over eight pounds instead of ten. When I released him back into the water, another cheer went up. The fifteenth hole was turning into a party. The old lady who gave me the Titleist balls kissed me so deeply I could taste Geritol. That party really took off. About an hour later, the course president was being shuttled out to the scene. His face was so red by the time he got there and you could hear him screaming from a hundred yards away. When he got to the hole, everyone scattered like cockroaches struck by the sudden light of a refrigerator door opening. I knew this was it. The green was torn up. The veins in the president's head were throbbing an oxygen-depleted purple. He jumped out of the cart pretty good for someone who was a hundred-and-two. Sure enough, he was spouting the sanctity of the game speech chapter and verse. I looked at John. He was looking at the ground in his best penitent sinner way. I could just feel that he was thinking about a way to save this. I was at the point where I didn't want to be saved. I had just landed Walter. I was feeling that wonderful high that only fly bums can really know. I thought if it ended here it would be a good ending. We could have dragged it on and hemmed and hawed until we received a letter in the mail citing some decision that concluded that our membership would not be renewed.

I shouted, "Go fuck yourself! You old cocksucker!"

I added the cocksucker just to ensure we were done. I could see the look come across John's face. I had sabotaged any argument.

It didn't take long for John to forgive me. John's game had advanced enough so that he could start losing to his bosses and they would feel good about it. We were back to barbeque and bullshit in no time. In a few short months, John would be gone. He suffered the fate of the corporate climber. It is well known that IBM stands for I've Been Moved. John was moved. As it happens, we swore we would keep in touch, but we drifted away. I'd like to think he is vice president at some soulless Fortune 500 company. That he has a condo in Hilton Head; I believe that is the dream.

I think the Walter Hagen bass was the event that released me from the spell of golf-course fishing. In all the years since I have not had the urge. Until this past June when I had a call from a good friend. He owns a local business and hosts a charity golf tournament for breast cancer. I have become very sensitive to cancer causes since being diagnosed with it. It's funny how that works. I wish I had been more sensitive before. It is a growth thing. I told Rick that I would indeed support the tournament. I have supported it in past years but have never golfed. This year's, he informed me, was at Shady Lake Country Club. My left eye began to twitch.

"Oh yeah?" I said. "Let me see if I can find my old clubs." I proceeded to search the catacombs under my house and indeed they were still there. I had always wanted to take a shot at Shady Lake. You could see the giant fish rises from the road. I figured I would just walk around looking golf-appropriate and fish the lake. It was a charity event on a Friday—who would care?

"That's a very interesting golf bag you have," Rick said when he was over at my house. He knew me long enough to know what I was up to. "Where do you want me to drop you off?"

"Any one of the back ponds," I replied. "Pick me up after lunch, I really want a crack at the big Shady."

Rick dropped me off at a little pond on the back nine. I looked at him inquisitively and he smiled back. He must have peeked into the water. I had a whale of a morning. It was silly. Every cast produced a bass or bluegill or sunfish. All big and willing. All acting like they had never seen a fly before. These were not quite ten-pound brook trout but I was flirting with nirvana anyway.

A little after lunch Rick came by in his golf cart. He was smiling. "So?"

"I should look into joining here," I said.

"Good luck," he said with a laugh.

"Yeah, yeah, I know. Let's see what the big lake has for me."

Rick dropped me off near a shady spot on Shady Lake. It fished nearly as well as the pond except the fish were bigger. As the afternoon wore on, things got better. It was almost the magic hour. That time just when the sun starts to go down. Twilight time is game time. It was the earliest shades of twilight when Rick came out. "I am done for the day," he said. "Are you staying?"

"It's just starting to get amazing. I can walk back to my car." As I was getting ready to say goodbye to my friend I saw a golf cart speeding toward us. I stared intently at the coming cart. "Could it be?" I thought. My suspicions were confirmed. Standing in front of me in his familiar shade of magenta was the president. "*You! You! You!*" he sputtered.

"Yeah it's me. Holy shit, you're still around. You must be a hundred-and-thirty! "

Rick was smiling. "I see you two know each other."

The president stammered at Rick, pointing the gnarled finger at me, "He called me a cocksucker!"

Rick looked at me. "I heard that he did."

Then I said a bit more, because I wanted to have more fun. "You really have to be careful. If you do it even once you *can* get a reputation." Now he really sputtered and spit. He began the familiar rant about the sanctity of the game. Rick, who was a valued member, began to smooth the guy over. In a weird déjà vu way, I was feeling a tug of nostalgia. Rick promised to take me away. I put my big golf bag in the cart. The president was still lecturing about the sanctity and honor of the game. I smiled and waved goodbye.

"How do you know him?" Rick asked.

"I knew him in another lifetime," I said. "He was a hundred-and-two then. I can tell you that he still hasn't lost his charm."

"Did you really call him a cocksucker?"

"Yeah, but you had to be there to appreciate it."

"What in the world could have happened for you to do that?"

"It's hard to explain. It was over Walter Hagen."

"Really?" You could see Rick's brow furrow. "Walter Hagen?"

"You never can tell what will set some people off."

A few weeks later Rick came over. We talked and laughed about the tournament. Rick told me that the president took a week off over the incident. We laughed about that for a bit.

"I guess you won't be fishing in next year's tournament," Rick said.

"The thing is," I replied, "I had to quit just before the magic hour. I have to get there to fish it if only once."

"I am pretty sure the president was serious about the 'over his dead body' thing."

"As tempting as that may be to wait, I do plan on being there for your tournament next year."

Rick's look was inquisitive. I told him to hang on as I left the room. I went to the closet in my bedroom. I was so pleased and smug. I began to round up all the elements of my plan. I pulled up a pair of shorts. I strapped on a large pre-filled bra. (I'm a big guy so I really had no problem pulling off the Double D's.) I pulled on a light pink polo; it was mostly polyester but with just enough elastane. I pulled up a tan golf skirt. My sneakers were pink and tan and tied together the ensemble so nicely. To top it all off, I donned a big blonde wig and some face-covering sunglasses. As I strutted into the den, I nearly killed Rick. It took a while for him to stop choking, and then to stop laughing.

"Oh my God," Rick giggled with tears running down his face. "Where did you get that get up?!"

"I picked up most of it for a Halloween party a few years back. The old bastard will never recognize me in this."

"He'll want to date you. It is unbelievable, you could pass for an LPGA pro anywhere."

"I'll offer to show him my putter. That ought to take care of him for good."

I am looking forward to golfing this year's tournament incognito. It is all in the spirit of fun. Part of me understands the president. Another part of me has some sympathy for him as well. I don't have the intense dislike for golfers that I used to. In fact, some of my best friends golf. The game is still intensely bloated and arrogant but it does accommodate some fine fishing. Many country clubs have a house pro. I think it would go a long way to a better image if some would entertain the idea of a course fly guy. I would surely volunteer.

Blades of Grass

A blade of grass is the journeywork of the stars.

—*Walt Whitman*

Bamboo fly rods—it is with a certain fascination and reverence that many flyfishers approach these blades of grass.

Bamboo is a wild and special grass. The most sought-after is the kind grown in the Tonkin region of China. Despite much effort to domesticate the plant, it remains friendly, approachable, intriguingly wild. Like housecats. Maybe those qualities draw me to both—they must be appreciated on their own terms.

Fly fishing has injected itself culturally into my life. This culture, in my life, has two parts: I simplistically label them BR and AR. That stands for Before River and After River—River being the movie *A River Runs Through It*. Norman Maclean's novella was a soulful and beautiful recounting of how his life was marked in time by the wholesome and spiritual communion with nature through fly fishing. The baby boomers, always on the lookout for soul nourishment, saw a good translation of the book in Robert Redford's film, *A River Runs Through It,* in 1992. It took the astute marketing teams of certain companies to exploit their (the Baby

Boomers, that is) desire for a soul, which turned my sport of fly fishing into a high-end, elitist affair and now those of us who enjoyed the sport BR could barely stand the new guys or afford the equipment.

What does this have to do with bamboo fly rods? You cannot possibly separate the bamboo rod from the culture of fly fishing. You also cannot ignore the great schism of 1992, when our culture and the grass we use as a fishing tool were affected forever.

When I started fly fishing, the appeal of bamboo was simple. It was affordable, more so than some of the new "space age" stuff being whispered about. It also fit my holistic approach to fishing. As a young man in the late seventies and reading Robert M. Persig's book, *Zen and the Art of Motorcycle Maintenance*, I could apply a Zen philosophy to fly fishing. Of course, bamboo screamed Zen. Besides all that, some of the rods were works of art that managed to be beautiful in a metaphysical way. In context with the times, the arms race was happening at full tilt, mass production was the in thing, The Beatles broke up, clothing was being made entirely of plastics, and the leisure suit was the rage. I still have one of those with the tags on it, a dreamy rich Creamsicle orange. I never wore a leisure suit. That is on a short list of things from the seventies that I am proud of.

The 1970s was not an era of great reconciliation with nature. In June 1969, the Cuyahoga River burned in Ohio. The Cleveland-area river had burned before, but this time newly sophisticated news media exploited the tragedy for profit. The picture of the river that *Time* magazine had on its cover fueled sales of that magazine. Exploitation can have some good side effects. Raising awareness can lead to education and understanding. Up to this point, water pollution was viewed as a necessary by-product of industry. It was one of those things that came with prosperity. With nature getting an elevated profile from the water burning, people started asking some of the right questions: Is this bad for us? Can it make us sick? Can we run out of clean water? I know it seems funny now but corporate America was a sinister motherfucker and did what it could to increase profit margins. Much to the intense displeasure of corporations, the flaming river helped America enact the Federal Clean Water Act of 1972.

The history of the day influences the evolving culture. In those days, I entered the culture of fly fishing. Though all the related "stuff" influenced fly-fishing's culture—the flies, reels, line, art, vests, and the rest of the tools—the sport was defined by the rods. In my Zen approach, I grew to love bamboo. You fished with one rod, primarily. Mine was a garage-sale find: a thirty-dollar Payne. I didn't know about its legendary future status; I just knew it to be of a fine reputation.

The ultimate goal was to catch a fish on a rod you built and a fly you tied. I still want to take a rod-building class. My fear is that it will be like my fly tying (not so good). There is real art to both. A deftness and a touch that in the best cases make things come alive. Really, this is the defining feature of bamboo that makes it special. When it all comes together between the rod and the fly and the angler, a certain animation occurs. That is the magic the rodbuilder pours his heart into capturing.

I have a good friend who is a diamond cutter. I know his reputation is special. At times, a large odd-shape stone comes to him to be cut. I have known Mike to carry the stone for some time, and to take it out at random and unspecified times. There was one time when I had to ask him: "What the hell are you doing?"

"I had to see it!" he screams back. He screamed because we were courtside at a Brooklyn Nets game. Later he explained that he could feel the energy from the gem. That in his career, he "listens" to the stone. That this helps him decide how to cut the stone. In the end, he sent me a photo of it finished. The diamond was stunning. Mike wrote under the photo, "She has the fire she has wanted for a millennium." I think the best rodmakers are like that. They study and pray over the project. Contemplate the spine and the action. In creative love, they coax an intrinsic specie-specific memory—that the leaves of grass have a life memory of blowing in the wind. At that right time, magic happens.

For me, that magic moment is the real magnetism of bamboo. I spend time carefully choosing the rod. Then I spend, in some cases, hours matching the reel and line to the rod. Casting over and over on the grass. When I get the balance just right, I need to fish it. Experienced fly fishers know about this moment. It is when everything comes together like a lightning strike. In the briefest of moments time seems to slow. The magic of the animation is going to happen, you know it. Big medicine. The leaf of grass is going to impart the magic through the line and into the fly. If the fly is tied with the same kind of medicine, then things just get that much hotter. In the magic moment, the fly animates in a lifelike way and sets upon the water with the electricity of life. For a moment Geppetto imparts life into Pinocchio. In this magic moment, the electricity is a beacon, one that sends out a message to all available fish. It is a primordial trigger that the finny predator reacts to. When it all comes together just like that . . . is why I fish bamboo. It is rare and special. It cannot be obtained through mass production or via inorganic media. Many times, a master rodmaker misses the mark. It is a tragic disappointment when you take some master's work out and the rod is a dud. You cast and cast. It is a fine rod from a man who has imparted the magic before. Yet in spite of your will otherwise, nothing happens. Even with the right "stuff" there is no guarantee it will happen. You can find the magic one evening and go back the following evening, everything being comparable, and you get nothing. Despite all this, we keep plugging along.

The guys I fished with all figured this out. We were part of the quirky fraternal order of flyfishermen. We were down the line far enough to feel the history of our sport. We knew enough to seek out and try to form some kind of relationship with Lee Wulff. We understood he was fly-fishing royalty. We were college kids in the Catskills tromping all over hallowed ground. Talking and trying to get as much out of the older guys as we could. There were guys who remembered Theodore Gordon, Harry Darbee, and Sparse Grey Hackle. You could be standing in the Junction Pool in Roscoe, New York, talking with someone whose memory went all the way back. You could stop at Dette's and buy flies from the same shop as the "greats." The history was linear and unbroken. I remember a sign next to a pickup truck just outside of Roscoe that read "Rust in Peace." It really is the mantra of the BR folks.

There is a parlor game called Six Degrees of Kevin Bacon. It is based on the six-degrees-of-separation concept, which posits that any two people on Earth are six or fewer acquaintance links apart. In this game, movie buffs challenged each other to find the least amount of links between any actor and the prolific Hollywood actor Kevin Bacon. In those early days we certainly could have played the six degrees of Lee Wulff. The challenge would have been to find the shortest path of people who had fished with Lee. Of course many people would consider fishing several pools away, and a friendly wave, fishing with Lee. In the "rust in peace" attitude, that would be okay. The point is that our sport, fly fishing, was really a close-knit community. It was a culture that formed around the communion with nature and the camaraderie of the magic that was unique to our thing.

In a moment, our sport changed forever. Norman Maclean was no stranger to us. His novella, *A River Runs Through It*, was talked about. It really captured a sense of the sport and the sports of fly fishing. It had a soulful message—that our sport could mark the seasons of a lifetime without malice. That we lived as part of the culture of magic. That in so many ways, in concurrence with life, that was enough. It spoke to living well. It was inevitable that Hollywood would get at it. Looking back, I wished it was done poorly. To Robert Redford's credit, he captured the flavor of the magic of our thing. At the same time, the baby-boom generation dominated the landscape. Their parents, who were part of the generation that Tom Brokaw aptly dubbed The Greatest Generation, ruined them. That "greatest generation" took a nation that was broken by the Depression and tempered in the greatest power struggle of our time, rose above everything, and built the greatest nation the planet had ever seen. In their zeal to fix everything, they gave their children, the boomers, everything. They inadvertently spoiled them for life. The boomers were given everything and without the discipline of their parents. This created an inferiority, a real hole in their soul. They did whatever they could to fill it. They used all the drugs they wanted, they all gorged themselves on conspicuous consumerism, all to try to feel better about life. When the movie came out, the locusts were ready to consume the next good thing.

We had no idea what was coming. Most of us didn't. There were a few who could smell it in the wind. They were part of the horrible generation and had marketing degrees. They knew their prey. They followed them like the buffalo hunters followed the buffalo. It was their mission to take the money out of the boomer pocket. They came out of the movie theaters with their faces all aglow. Fly fishing was going to fill the hole in the soul. Overnight, there were catalogs filled with expensive rods, reels, clothing, nets, all kinds of shit I had never heard of. Everything was getting endorsed. This experience was so far out of anything they (the boomers) had known, they needed guidance. Boy did they get it.

Those of us around BR were witnessing the invasion of our sport. Great numbers sprung up around us. We had no clue what was happening. All of a sudden, where we fished became crowded with rude people; the equipment we used we no longer could afford at new prices. Our quaint little sport was run over.

Personally, I hung onto the people I knew and the equipment I had. I tried to keep on doing what I had always done. Supply and demand started to come into play. There was no way bamboo-rod makers were going to keep up. This caused a major inflation in prices. Even worse, a new term came into existence: "Investment Grade Bamboo Rods." This left me with one question: where were the "Fishing Grade Bamboo Rods?" This shortfall led to a huge production of synthetic rods. This wasn't all bad; some very nice rods came on the market. Companies such as R. L. Winston, Sage, and G. Loomis tried to bring a sense of the old-time craftsmanship to the industry. I have grown very fond of the Winston IM6 rods. I do fish graphite. I love bamboo but there are times when graphite just makes more sense.

Instantly, the AR group added a little water and had instant culture. It had nothing to do with the old historical truth of fly fishing. It was created. Fishable bamboo became scarce. The old guard held onto theirs. (Although some succumbed to the big money being thrown at them.) It was almost with regularity that someone would see your bamboo and come up to give you their thoughts on it. Once, I was fishing a fine Sweetwater. I consider George Maurer's rods with the highest regard. Without being asked or having any regard for my feelings, an AR rod expert came up to me, interrupting my fishing to tell me that the rod I was fishing was a piece of shit. He proceeded to lecture to me that if I could not afford (he kept looking at my multiple patched Simms waders) a decent Leonard, that he would be glad to give me the 1–800 number to Orvis. I probably shouldn't have done it. It was the wrong thing to do and really fucked with my Zen program of fly fishing. What I did is reach down into the streambed for a nice rock. I found one that seemed to have been put there by the fishing gods—I mean by the way it fit perfectly into the palm of my hand. No baseball ever felt so at home in my grasp. His head was such an ample target. It was a dumb thing to do and it did complicate my life—no matter how good it felt at the time. I know it doesn't sound like I am sorry. Maybe, after all, I'm not.

It was like that for quite a while. Two separate cultures running parallel along the same sport. The old guys being and acting old school. The new guys exerting their ideas about the sport. Somehow they got by for a while in the status-symbol game. They would show up streamside with new outfits as the catalogs dictated. It wasn't all bad. They injected tons of money. Manufacturers did well. There were big advertising budgets. It fueled a media expansion. We had more magazines, television shows, and tons of social media. More important, bamboo again began to be made in a cottage way. New and exciting rodmakers threw their hats into the ring. The real problem was that the boomers didn't have the patience to find the real magic of the sport. It was not the instant fix they were looking for. Like the locusts they are, they came, they consumed, and they left.

Some did stick around. It is my theory that some of these guys started fooling around with bamboo and stumbled on the magic. There are probably as many AR guys left as there are BR guys left. The funny thing is that there is now plenty of bamboo for everyone. Sounds like everything is great but it is not.

Our sport—or, rather, the industry around our sport—is in trouble. The buffalo are all gone. Maybe that isn't such a bad thing. I am fond of the local fly shops and hope they hold on. We are sailing into some new waters.

In the end, all we can do is our best. Support our local fly shops and go and drop a few bucks at a lodge or two a year. Keep an interest in helping the nonprofits that help us. Vote for the guys who give us clean and ample water full of wild fish. Buy bamboo rods and fish them hard. Keep the magical ones and sell the duds to collectors (they'll never know). Preserve our history. Most important: rust in peace.

Squirrel Stew

The idea is that there is a kind of memory
in nature. Each kind of thing has a collective
memory. So, take a squirrel living in New
York now. That squirrel is being influenced
by all past squirrels.

—*Rupert Sheldrake*

In the natural cycles of outdoor activity there is, by way of natural law and the laws of men, a lull. It is really the hard times between the end of the harvest and the rebirth of spring. In some places, the laws have been changed to offer a broader window of opportunity. For example, in my home state of New York, squirrel-hunting season now extends a whole month past when everything else is over and closed.

I tend to read a lot. I have a library with a bunch of books I love. If you walk into it, you would come away with the feeling that I might be a geek. Of course, that would only be partially true. I also like to buy many magazines. Then there are times when I cruise the internet looking for new ideas. New ideas are hard to come by. With Earth's population exploding to almost eight billion, the chances of having an original thought are very slim. Of course I have other interests. My latest session of internet cruising was searching out tickets and friends for the last Grateful Dead show. The "Fare Thee Well" shows were scheduled on July 3, 2015 (my son's first birthday; I missed that concert), and July 4 and 5. I will probably make the one on the fifth after paying some crazy money for the tickets. I figure I came in with them, I may as well see them out. I spent most of my life in the counterculture. Twenty-eight years on the road with George Carlin allowed me to keep it going on. Of course now I am a relic, of sorts. I like the ideals of that era. Peace, Love, and Balance. All the things Big Brother hates. Am I sounding like a faded, old tie-dye? I still even wear tie-dye, when I can. I was lucky enough to live this way my whole life. I am proud to say I was never a corporate tool.

In this mixture of being a geek, hippie, trout bum, sporting enthusiast, and entropist I tend to find stuff that most people overlook. Oftentimes by their own desire. In the grasp of boredom induced by a Central-Western, New York, winter, I came across a quasi-biologist named Rupert Sheldrake. (Sorry about the quasi part, Rupert.) He has come up with a theory called "morphic resonance." The concepts within morphic resonance become quite detailed. They are biological theories with overtones of Lamarckian ideas of acquired characteristics being passed on as inherited traits. It is interesting and complex and when he used the example of a squirrel in New York having inherited a collective knowledge from all it past generations, my eyes lit up. I live in New York and my life path has crossed the paths of the New York squirrels in question. I could, at least in a small way, test out old Rupert's theory.

As I was working it out, if Rupert's theory was true, the squirrels that I hunted many years ago would have passed down the exploits of the legendary squirrel hunter—me. In my younger days, I really enjoyed squirrel hunting. It has been quite a while since I pulled a trigger on one. Why did I stop hunting them? It was because of my belief system. I do not kill anything I won't use. The problem with squirrels is really not me. I love to eat them. I have a recipe for squirrel stew that is just delicious. It is getting the people around me to eat them. I used to feed it to my daughters when they were too young to know what the hell was in the stew. As my family figured out what was in the stew, they refused it. When I first started this type of hunting, squirrels were considered good table fare. I was a self-taught hunter coming from a family who didn't believe in guns; I tended to hunt with some of the older sports around at the time. They had a more holistic view. If something was what they ate, what could be better to eat than a squirrel? There is truth to that. The diet of a squirrel is almost entirely seeds. They gave me some great stew recipes. Finding recipes for squirrels can be tough—in fact finding good game recipes in general can be a chore. One of the things I found out years ago is to pay attention to cookbooks at garage sales. If they have recipes written in or attached, I buy them. One of my other loves is cooking. I have come across some family "secret recipes" in used cookbooks. In my mind those are true treasures. Here's one:

SQUIRREL STEW
    2 squirrels
    6 tablespoons butter
    6 to 8 teaspoons flour
    Salt and pepper to taste (I prefer white pepper)
    1 cup sifted high-quality flour
    2 teaspoons baking powder
    ¼ teaspoon salt
    1 tablespoon shortening
    6 tablespoons milk

Boil the cleaned squirrels in water with enough salt and pepper (this is your stew, you know what enough

means for you). Boil until the meat pulls easily from
the bone. Take the meat from the bones and place in a
bowl. Discard the bones. Add butter and flour mixture,
slowly, to the boiling water. Return the meat to the
water or the pre-stew liquid. You pick what you want
to call it. In another container, stir the larger quantity of
flour, baking powder, and ¼ teaspoon of salt. Add short-
ening and pinch it in with your fingers until it squeals
or is well mixed. Gradually stir in milk, little by little
until it is soft. You might not use all the milk. If not,
just drink the rest. Drop the dumplings you have created carefully into the stew. I use a slotted spoon. Add
more water if needed for the dumplings to float above
the meat, and cook well. Cook until the dumplings are
done, about fifteen to twenty minutes. This is very tasty
with toast or garlic toast. Also goes very well with a fine
single malt Scotch.

After reading the recipe, it does sound as if this might be tasty—
and it is. The thought of visiting the state forest that was my traditional squirrel grounds had me a bit excited. There is a spot I love.
You hike about a mile in from the forest road. There is a beautiful
stand of planted pines—I know they are planted because they are
in perfect rows. The canopy has grown high enough so you can
stand in the stand of trees. Below your feet is a carpet of years of
falling needles. In your bare feet it might be painful, but in boots
it is a cushy, quiet, luxurious stroll.

    It was funny strolling through the old forest. Some things
had changed but not many. There used to be a deadfall of a very
large oak. (Did you ever really consider trees? I mean, in terms of
the cycle of life. Maybe because it is so seldom that we are able to
see a tree at the end.) This was a massive oak that as far as I could
tell died of old age. It has been at least two decades since I was in

this forest. I used to come here with a dear friend. Dave Haines was about as gentle a soul as I ever knew. In the time we knew each other and our lives intersected, life was simpler. We were mostly broke and hunted and fished to place food on our tables. Good food. We had enough money to afford spaghetti and a jar of Ragu. We really didn't have enough for, say, trout amandine. Unless we caught and killed the trout ourselves and played cook.

I had found the massive oak. It was still on its side and, apart from some mossy growth, looked the same. My memory recalled the time I carved a seat in the oak that made a good and comfortable spot. In a moment I was sitting in that very spot and it still felt good. The main difference was my ass was spilling over the edges that I had carved. Time will do that. I, for a moment, thought about taking out my Buck knife and expanding the seat a couple inches. I didn't. It was sort of like keeping that really faded pair of jeans that are tight. Ah, nostalgia.

As I sat in the seat on the oak, I could feel the tide of past memories come flooding around me. I recalled the last time Dave and I were here. It was a sunny fall day when my hair had no gray. We were hunting squirrels for a nice red-sauce recipe I had put together for pasta. We would try to put something nice together for Sunday dinners. At about this time in life we were both pumping gas for Hi-Way Oil. It was a full-service station so we actually pumped the gas, checked your oil, and washed your windows. If we were pleasant enough and earnest about the windows, we might grab an extra buck as a tip. It was easy to take your tip money to Jake's Tavern. Jake's was a watering hole in the little town of Laurens, N.Y., where Dave lived. It was something of an anomaly back then; really, it would be impossible today. Recalling the place still brings a smile to my face. It was owned by two brothers who lived above the bar. They were a bit odd and the décor of the place reflected it. As you walked in, the first thing that caught your eye was the large antique oak bar. As your eyes adjusted, you noticed that the walls had old barn wood as a wainscoting that went halfway up the wall. Above the wainscoting was gold foil wallpaper with red velvet *fleur-de-lis* as a pattern that repeated every four inches. Around the bar were crystal wall sconces and between them were various animal heads, and alternating with the heads were ballerina prints by Pál Fried. Then off to one side was a pool table covered in a purple felt. If by now your mind's eye is full of a fashion nightmare—then you have the flavor of Jake's.

In spite of itself, the place had a certain charm. Dave and I were members of the "mug club." For five dollars you were given a glass mug and an electric etching pen. You applied your name and whatever else you felt like, and the mug was yours. You left it at the bar and used it when you showed up and this entitled you to 75-cent drafts.

I hadn't thought about Jake's in a long time. The nostalgia of the moment put a lump in my throat. I missed Dave. I know some guys seem to have a whole tribe of fishing and hunting buddies. I really only had two.

I sat in the seat waiting for nature to resume its affairs. When you walk into the woods, everything there knows. You try to be quiet and go slow—which does help up to a point, but man in general is clumsy and smelly by wilderness standards. It mostly means that you have to sit perfectly still for a while and nature will resume what it does. For squirrel hunting, it usually takes about half an hour, sometimes less. I find it easy to sit still these days. In my youth it was pure torture. I think now I have enough memories to recall so I can fill the time. Sitting on the oak deadfall, I was remembering more time spent with Dave.

The best memory was the time we went to the Adirondacks together. Dave's band The Voltz had a gig in Whitehall, New York. This was about the time states were raising the drinking age. At times, one neighboring state might have a lower age. The state with the younger drinking age benefited. It was like that between New York and Vermont. Dave was the drummer and on rare occasions they would let me sit in with the band. Whitehall was near the Adirondacks, so of course we decided to go early and do some fall fishing. When we got to Raquette Lake, we filled the canoe with ice, two cases of beer, snacks, chips, a shotgun, and camping and fishing equipment. We were planning to spend two nights at a lean-to campground. We fished from the boat launch to the campground. It was fall; I remember because it was also duck season. The fishing was very good and I remember hooking a large smallmouth bass. I fought it for quite some time and Dave tried to lift the fish by the leader, and the line and fish parted company. By that time, it was well past dark and we decided it might be prudent to set up camp. That night was like so many we had. Fire roaring, cold beer, and talking. There was a real quality to the conversations. I think the art of conversation is almost gone. It has suffered from the decline of alcohol consumption by roaring fires.

Young men often overlook the value of good nutrition and can get by with beer and corn chips. That menu served us that night. In time, the fire burned to a bed of glowing embers and sleep crept in. Morning came with the sound of ducks frolicking yards away. The thought of chips for breakfast was rejected. Quietly, I slipped down to the water's edge and dispatched two mallards. I cleaned them right there and washed them in the cool Adirondack waters. I pushed the embers from the previous night's fire together to coax a new and steady heat. It was not long before the delicious smell of roasting ducks disturbed Dave's sleep. He woke and came to the fire. We sat quietly, both thankful that breakfast was not beer and chips. The grease from the ducks dripped onto the hot embers, causing the occasional flare up. It wasn't long before the ducks were cooked. Something about the aroma of the roasting birds and the fall air, combined with our hunger, made that breakfast one of the best I ever had.

Devour is a word that is seldom used correctly. It is really about a meal that comes in a timely fashion enhanced with a real hunger. We devoured those roasted ducks in a way I still recall today. So delicious.

That day we fished the lake and the confluence where the river came in. It was one of those fall days when the feed is on—when nature rings the dinner bell. All the fish feed frantically to put on that last bit of fat that will hold them over in harsh Adirondack winters. If you can catch the "last" feeding frenzy, you are lucky. After that it slows down and fishing becomes spotty.

The fishing was a smorgasbord and every hookset was a mystery: Trout, bass, yellow perch, and Pike were all on offer. We decided to keep the yellow perch for dinner. Back at the camp-ground we used what we had on hand: fillets dredged in beer and coated in potato-chip crumbs. It was a tasty dinner. Fresh fish is perhaps the hardest meal to fuck up. Thankfully. Around the fire that evening, we discussed the following day's plan. We reasoned that the launch was a half-hour paddle away. If we stopped fishing at three, we would have plenty of time to make the gig. Time is a funny and fluid thing. When you are young it seems more forgiving and manageable.

The old adage "red sky in the morning, sailors take warning" rumbled around in my head that next morning. We broke camp and discussed the coming clouds. Our consensus was that it would take most of the day to come to us. I have always had good fishing on a falling barometer. I didn't need a gauge to feel the barometric pressure crashing around us. At the same time, the fishing was just becoming unbelievable. We were hitting doubles with regularity. But the clouds that seemed so far away just a few hours ago became much closer.

"Dave," I said, "you think we should get going?" At that moment my rod was doubled over with a heavy fish.

"Huh?" Dave answered. "Naw, it'll be fine."

It was almost as if the conversation was an annoyance as his rod was also pulling on a heavy fish. They say things come in threes. I really don't know about that. I do know that afternoon the wind grew stronger, the white caps rose higher, and the fishing got hotter; the perfect convergence of a quandary. As I released a fat bass, a whitecap broke over the canoe. It drenched me and therefore caught my full attention.

"Dave, I really think we need to get going!" I now implored.

"Are you kidding? We have at least an hour." Dave was so gung ho.

"What direction is the launch?" I had gotten turned around a bit.

"Ummm?" It seemed Dave was turned around too.

I had to take out my compass. I had reoriented and I pointed to the direction of the launch—the same direction the now gale-force winds were coming from.

"Hey, does it seem like the boat launch is a lot farther away?" Dave commented.

While we were sorting this out, we still were fishing and catching big fish. At the same time, water was breaking over the canoe gunnels and starting to fill the bottom of the boat. It had finally reached a volume that caused us to put up our rods, bail the boat, and then start paddling toward the launch. At first we paddled at a steady rate . . . but it was very slow going. A look at our watches showed time was a concern. The harder we paddled, the harder the wind blew. Almost three hours later we reached the shore. In a very quick pace we stowed the gear and had the canoe on the roof of the vehicle. It was my vehicle, a poor little Volkswagen Sirocco. I reached up to turn the key over and started to cry.

"Why are you crying?" Dave said through his own sobbing and tears. I just looked at him. Both our arms were on fire from paddling so furiously. We were late for the gig and I was driving mountain roads. Every turn caused more tears. We arrived in the parking lot an hour late with Dave's bandmates waiting and pacing. We tried to get out of playing but the rest of the guys would have none of it. The deposit from the bar owner was long spent. Dave and I both wore sunglasses. We weren't trying to be cool; we didn't want people to see our tears.

When we started playing, we slowed everything down. I recall a bloated, twenty-five minute version of "Stairway to Heaven." We ended up spending the night sleeping in my little car. The next day we purchased a few tubes of BenGay pain-relief ointment to ease the soreness in our arms and forced-marched ourselves home. We went back to that campground the next year and carved our initials into the lean-to. Over the years, we recounted that story often.

Sitting on that old oak tree I wondered if our initials were still there. It has been about a quarter of a century since the day Dave lost control of his big, old Cadillac. The call informing me of his death stung me to my heart. I have these wonderful memories of our days afield. I can tell you I still miss him. The sound of rustling leaves carried me back to here and now.

A big squirrel is rooting around under the fallen canopy of leaves looking for the acorn he missed earlier. Over my left shoulder comes more rustling. I look up to see the squirrels running the canopy. Watching them jumping from branch to branch overhead is something that amuses me. They can be true acrobats. It is also my favorite method of harvesting them. It seems more sporting than taking them off the ground. It may be the prejudices of the bird hunter in me. I could have taken two squirrels quickly and easily. If Sheldrake's theory of morphic resonance does exist it was not evident with these particular squirrels. It might be argued that I wasn't as legendary a squirrel hunter as I credited myself to be, and that my influence was unremarkable and therefore a nonfactor. I have a hard time accepting that. It must be that this particular population of squirrels is minimally exceptional.

I took my time sitting there and enjoying the ambiance. Nostalgia is a funny thing. It is often bittersweet and always very personal. Its usefulness is about feeling the quality of our lives. In time the undersized "seat" started to hurt my ass and I picked out two plump squirrels to shoot. On the drive home, I wandered through more memories. Eventually I was home enjoying the smell of the stew simmering. I was thinking about how I enjoyed that afternoon and wondering if I would ever go back. I pulled two bowls from the cupboard. I ladled a nice hearty bowl for me. I set the other bowl across the table and, not liking to waste anything, I carefully placed a couple of tablespoons of squirrel stew in it. It was there for the memory of my friend Dave.

My October Browns

I'm so glad I live in a world where there
are Octobers.
—*L. M. Montgomery, Anne of Green Gables*

Sometimes we have magic right under our noses. In familiarity, and due to constant human contact and interaction, we can forget it is magic. For many years, I had an office in Niagara Falls, New York. People would always say, "So you must go to the Falls all the time?"

The truth was—no, I did not. I would drive by often getting and giving no more than a glimpse. As for actually going there to see the Falls, that was reserved for visiting guests who wanted to see the attraction. On those trips, I would realize all over again why this was one of the natural wonders of the world. What if I told you there was a place from which you could sight cast for big brown trout and that it was entirely possible to catch ten of them over ten pounds in a single day? That it would be during the magnificent fall foliage in the perfectly cool days of October? Indeed, it is that special kind of magic of which I'm speaking. That is the thrill I face each fall in the south shore tributaries of Lake Ontario, in New York State.

In the fall, these tributaries start to receive waves of migrating fish. First come the Pacific salmon coho (silvers), and the Chinook (kings). They come to spawn and their eggs attract the egg-eating species like steelhead and Atlantic salmon and even the odd lake trout. Around the end of September and building to a crescendo around Halloween, the brown trout come to spawn. The expansive freshwater Great Lakes and their tributaries hold megatons of baitfish. The browns feast all through the summer and arrive in pristine condition. They come from the lake wearing a silver sheen, but it falls away quickly. In its place are the spawning colors that go step-by-step with the fall foliage. The fish all have very broad shoulders and massive, sweeping tails. To find one under 4 pounds would be a challenge; to find one more than 20 pounds would not be. In the heat of the pressing sexual urges, the very large fish are available and you can sight cast for them. If you are lucky enough, the fishing equivalent of "buck fever"—what I call "brown fever"—lights up and your casting begins to flow.

There are the true trout bums. Those souls that in one way or another can dedicate all their time to fishing. I share the gypsy soul with them but as of yet I have not thrown off all the trappings of responsibility. Although I have managed to be in a place in which I can frame my time, I do have to work. The bills keep coming. I have to slay the dragons of the business in which I endeavor to make a living. I have managed to slip past the time clock and cheat the rat race, just a little. It just means that I will go in to the office late tomorrow. I will get up before first light. I will gather my things—but in two sets. One set will outfit me for the few hours of fishing I will steal in the morning; the other for the business meetings I must attend afterward.

The gathering of our stuff to prepare for the day on the water is often curious. We try to forecast our needs. We add things to piles and arrange them and redo them until we have a blend of practical and useful artifacts we think we will need—an educated guess with an eye toward the conservation of space. It usually works. Some guys make lists, but those are for the rookies and the stupid.

I try to have myself all together by the 11:00 p.m. news. With all the weather sites available on the super information highway, the local news still is the best indicator of the local weather. Where I live in Central New York, the format of the local news has remained unchanged for many years. I like that. It is devoid of all the heavy political influence that the cable news channels carry. I cannot stand cable news. In years gone by, we used to have a half-hour of the local news followed by a half-hour of national news. Even then, at times not much either happened or was reported. Then they would scramble for those cute, human-interest stories such as where Fluffy walked 387 miles to be reunited with her master. Now they manage to fill the air 24/7. It is a pile of shit and you need to be careful or the tail will wag the dog. I watch the eleven o'clock news and nothing else. I am much happier for it.

I am not sure anymore who has evening rituals and who does not. In my family, we have been going on for generations. I suspect these rituals are more common than not. I go and check all the door locks. Then I take my medicine. This has not always been part of the routine—the big white pill and the little pink ones. The rest come with the morning routine. I then go over my appointments for the following day. I like a couple of cookies and a glass of milk. Some things are just holdovers from a childhood during which cookies and milk were the ultimate comfort foods. Wash your face and brush your teeth and whatever hygiene is needed. The last act would be to set the alarm clock.

In the morning, the shrill beeping of the alarm disrupts my slumber. I think about the snooze button. The temptation is great.

I am a procrastinator by nature and a resleep button on an alarm clock is a pathway to procrastination. I have often thought about replacing it with an alarm clock without the snooze button. Then I recall those very cold winter mornings on which the breach created in the warm cocoon by my arm reaching for the snooze button lets a stream of cold air come rushing under the blankets. The goose bumps that the cold causes egg me on to hit the snooze button. The blanket breach, once repaired, stops the cold air and the heat quickly reestablishes and sleep washes over me once more. Something about those bouts of sleep feels so good. I never want to let that go. There will come a day on which I hit the snooze button for hours. The act will be my thesis in procrastination. Not today. I am going fishing. A desire that is greater than the procrastination contemplation.

The act of getting up is usual. The moment that lingers is the one in which I swing my legs over the edge of the bed. While my legs dangle and my toes reach for the floor, I take stock. I see how I feel. How gradually over the years, the dangling proposition of the day has changed. Then I shift my weight forward and my toes feel the floor. In an easy moment, I stand up out of bed. The day has begun. I start to move at a brisk pace. I begin the morning ritual, which is similar to the evening one. Eventually, I am out the door and on my way to the river.

I approach the turnoff near one of my favorite spots. Today I will fish Oak Orchard. It is a well-known spot and can be crowded. Today is a weekday so I know there will be room for me. I get out of my car and go 'round to the trunk. As I open it to reach for my waders, I draw a deep breath of air. It is cool, crisp, and sweet. The leaves on the trees are turning. The landscape is awash with yellows and reds and oranges. The air is maybe 50 degrees and the grass is heavy with dew.

You draw a deeper breath through your nose and you feel your sinuses shrink, making it possible to draw even deeper volumes of air into your lungs. You think about how fall is the best season. You linger on the sweetness your nose and palate taste. It is from the cold nights fixing the sugar in the flora. You feel more alive and younger than you are. Putting on the waders and stringing up the pretty 6-weight bamboo is a pleasure. You are invigorated.

You approach the river slowly. You see two fishermen almost 300 yards apart. It will be easy to slip into a spot somewhere between them. You look very carefully at the water. The morning will be short. Meetings await in the afternoon. Your eyes sweep back and forth. Finally you see it—a powerful tail moving the gravel by sweeping back and forth. You look closer to make sure it is not a salmon. Moments later you detect the flash of mustard yellow. This signals brown trout. The stalk begins.

I looked over the best path to take to get in the right spot. I kept my eyes riveted on the fish, a big buck brown trout. I lifted and set each foot carefully. *Wooosh!* This elicited an audible sound from me. Halfway between a scream and a shout. I was staring so intently that I nearly stepped on a bedded king salmon, which in turn scared the shit right out of me. The other fishermen were amused but knew the feeling. I stood there with my heart pounding like a drum. Eventually, I started to laugh. It is very similar to flushing a grouse in the snow. You get that sudden gush of adrenaline and then you laugh at the silliness of it. It is unavoidable. It has happened before and will happen again.

After I had gotten into place, I studied the fish for a bit. Settling in always shows you more. I could see the hen. Thirty feet past this lie was another brown preparing his breeding spot. The urge for sex is powerful in all things. It draws a certain intensity from the entities preparing to create life. The distraction is useful for a flyfisherman like me. This buck was at least 10 pounds and I was getting all jittery. A friend gave me a hideous fly. He called it Frankenstein. It was a size 8 Woolly Bugger with a mottled green-and-purple body. The head was a gold bead with little red eyes painted on it. It was grotesque, and with Halloween coming, appropriate. I tied on the fly. Out of the corner of my eye, I watched the trout. Eventually—and in spite of my shaking hands—I managed a good knot.

I always try to arrange my casts by starting a bit away and then coming closer with the next casts. I worked the Bugger methodically. I let it swing by and go well downstream before I pulled up the line and cast again. At this stage of the game, people like to speculate on what makes a spawning brown trout eat a fly, or any lure. Some feel it is a reflex based on the feeding instinct. Others feel it might be a reaction caused by aggressive spawning instincts. I can never decide which. The thing I do know is that some days they won't touch anything except a certain color pattern in a certain size. Other days they will pound anything near them. Mostly it is a variation between the two. With that kind of selectivity, it is hard to decide what and why they take. It is part of why I love this sport so. The mysteries are tantalizing and cracking the codes are satisfying—when you do.

One of my casts was working downstream, well past my intended target, when the fly was hit hard and fast. I love those strikes that jar you up into your shoulder. I set on the fish and immediately a beautiful and large smallmouth bass took flight. I was trying to keep her downstream; I wanted the commotion to be away from the intended quarry. I followed the bass some ways downstream. I beached the beauty after a wonderful fight. I remembered being annoyed when I first identified her but that didn't last. As I looked at her where I beached her, she was all of three pounds. She was green with an iridescent bronze glow. I released her quietly and felt joy that she chose to fight with me that morning.

As I waded back into the river, I saw a splash. A little farther out from me was a beautiful hen brown. Easily as big as the buck

I was casting to before. I waded a little bit to get a good angle on her. One of the best things about Great Lakes tributaries in the fall is that distractions come easy. I loaded my line and the cast was perfect.

As the fly began to swing near the golden beauty, she swam and took the fly. I pulled back and drove the hook into the corner of her mouth. She took off upstream like a mad woman. I was into my backing and my rod was deflecting the power of the fish.

This is the payoff: standing in a river on a beautiful fall morning tethered to a giant brown trout. In the fight, my eyes met those of the fisherman below me. He smiled back knowingly. To ask for more than this would be an insult. Eventually, I beached her in the same spot in which I beached the bass. I reached for the old scale I keep in my vest. It said she weighed a tad over 12 pounds. It is an old brass scale and could be off a bit, but ounces not pounds. I released her carefully. I felt for the pocket watch I keep in the big vest pocket. My fingers felt around and finally identified the watch by touch. I drew it out and opened the cover over the face. The old and ornate hands told me I had to go.

At the car, I removed my waders and sweater. I straightened my tie and put on my shoes. In a few minutes, I went from fly-fisherman to businessman. As I drove back to the world, I searched the feelings in my heart. I was thinking about whether I would be back tomorrow.

These Octobers are truly magnificent. Sometimes you just do it because you are an outdoorsman and it is where you need to be. Sometimes it is like standing by the edge of Niagara Falls—that you have to stop and think of how special it is. As I sat in the business meeting, my mind wondered how many other meetings were going on in the world that day. It was easy to imagine that it was a rather large number. Then I wondered how many people in those meetings had caught a big smallmouth bass and giant brown trout before the meetings began. Not many.

Indian Summer Perch

> The Indian Summer, the dead Summer's soul.
>
> —*Mary Clemmer, from the poem "Presence"*

Indian summer is primarily a North American phenomenon. In fact, the term "Indian," in North American references, aside from being politically incorrect, can be downright confusing. Other cultures in the Northern Hemisphere also tried to express this time of year. In England during the nineteenth century, which was the heyday of the British Raj in the Indian subcontinent, the term Indian summer became erroneously affiliated with the country India. It was a reference to the misnomer of Native Americans.

Really, the origins of the term Indian summer are murky and unsure. Some believe that it goes back to Narragansett natives who felt that the late-in-the-year seasonal warm spell was sent to them from their southwestern God, Cautantowwit. Others believe it came from settlers in New England; it is said that those settlers looked forward to the cold weather of late October as they felt the natives would be too busy preparing for winter and they could leave their stockades unarmed and unmanned.

Predictably, a warming would occur and the Native Americans could have one last whack at the Colonists. It is said that settlers named it Indian summer as a native holiday and a time of colonial vigilance.

As uncertain as the origins are, the defining parameters of this time of year are even more confusing.

In their attempts to nail it down, to clarify what defines authentic Indian summer, people have come up with large and often contradictory lists. Some state that it must follow at least one major killing frost; others that it must exceed three, four, five, and on some lists six days; that it must be later than October thirty-first; that it must fall between November first and November twentieth; that it must start on St. Martins Day (November eleventh); that it must occur before January first; that there must be a hazy or smoky veil to the event; windless high barometer days with a chilled night where your breath must be visible while you clearly can see the harvest moon. Some even take a highly scientific route, believing that an advancing Arctic air mass gets converted into a big, warm, stationary anticyclonic system that can and should lead to the significant but necessary differentials between day temperatures and evening temperatures. I could go on as there are plenty more opinions on the matter. A surprising amount of bullshit defines a very pleasant event.

As for me, I shall not attempt further to define the criteria necessary to have an authentic Indian summer. I may never succeed in coming up with a clear and universally understood definition of Indian summer. What I can say about Indian summer is that I know it when I see it. I am sure that almost everyone in North America knows it when they see it. Supreme Court Justice Potter Stewart would be so proud!

Autumn is my favorite season. The calendar says it starts September twenty-first with the Autumnal Equinox, where day and night have the same duration. The last day of fall according to the calendar is December twenty-first. Nature, having little regard for our calendar, does what she will. In our neck of the woods in the Northeast, fall gives up the ghost and surrenders to winter usually before December twenty-first. My love of the fall comes from its nature and mine being similar. It is a gradual slowing of the vivacious living of the summer. The fast-growing grass and the general conversion of the sun's energy into life-sustaining sugars slows and approaches the dormancy of winter. This period offers cool, crisp days and cooler, crisper nights. It is when nature gives to us the finished bounty of her summer's work.

I love that the cornucopia is often the symbol of fall. A horn of plenty signifies the last bounty and in many cases the sweetest of the year. I like to think that the first Thanksgiving was a celebration of that deeply wired appreciation for the life sustenance that Mother Earth gives to us. Though the date for the holiday was eventually set by Congress, I believe it was consecrated during an Indian summer. Thanksgiving, by far, is my favorite holiday. It has resisted being fouled by corporate commercialism—barely, but it has. Black Friday may be the most honestly named day of the year. In one split second, we go from one of the most sincere and wholesome moments to total irreverence and exploitation.

I always love the opportunities the fall gives us to have personal experiences under the harvest moon. It is so deep within us that you must really be disconnected from your soul to avoid it. When I sit in my deer stand with my bow, I can feel the grace of Mother Earth. When I go into my garden to take the last tomatoes and squash, I feel it. When I arrive at a farmer's roadside stand and sort through the day's picked apples, I feel it. As the days shorten and the brightly-colored reds, yellows, and ochre leaves fall from the trees, I know the harsh spinster and her cold, prying fingers are coming. Winter lacks the subtlety of the other seasons. Spring yields to summer in a seamless joyous mood, and then summer gently welcomes autumn. Winter cooperates with no other season.

Indian summer is a spiritual promise that fall will return. It gives us one last chance to harvest in a backdrop of perfection. I write this as Indian summer has just left. She started on a Monday that had the cliché blue sky and seventy-something on the thermometer. When I was an apple farmer in a past life, I would wait for this time to pick the Granny Smith variety of apples. The later I could hold out, the sweeter those big green apples would be. I am always looking for some kind of last "harvest" to seal the deal of the summer in fall. As I was thinking about it—this false summer—I received a call from a close friend asking if we (my wife and I) wanted to catch dinner with him and his wife. I agreed.

The following evening, we met Rich and Lisa at a favorite restaurant. The dinner conversation turned, as it often does, to fishing. The funny thing is that we all love to fish but we seldom fish together. Rich is a partner in a chain of family restaurants and works far too hard. I will often get emails from him in the wee hours of the morning. The screwed-up part is that I am often awake and respond at 3:05 a.m. Rich has a manager at one of his restaurants named Paul Nagel. Aside from being a culinary resource engineer, he is a fishing guide. His title, "culinary resource engineer," reminds me how we use the English language to confuse communication. I recently encountered someone who told me her profession was modality manager. I shook my head as if I understood. Eventually the lights came on . . . a nurse! That gave me pause and cause to find other confusing job titles. Media Distribution Officer—that's a paperboy. Transparency Enhancement Facilitator—window cleaner. Director of First Impressions—receptionist.

This made me feel the need to help Paul with a title for his alternate occupation (his other job). All I could come up with was *Ichthyological* Procurement Specialist.

Rich received a text from Paul at dinner. It was a photo of a cooler full of jumbo yellow perch, what I learned in Central New York to call jack perch. I looked at Rich and I'm sure my eyes were all lit up. "Let's go!" I said. "When?" Rich replied. "Let's go tomorrow." I was excited. Here was my last Indian summer harvest opportunity.

Rich said, "I can't go. But I'll text him for you. I have meetings all day."

"Call in sick!" I said.

"I can't, we are opening that new dining room this week."

I said, "You are always busy. Come on, let's blow off work."

I was starting to feel like the bad influence. "You know the restaurants are not going to fold up the day after you die. They'll be open selling the world's greatest cheeseburgers with or without you."

Rich said, "I know. Paul just texted back, he can take you tomorrow."

"You know when you die you can't get these days back. It's going to be beautiful tomorrow. It's supposed to turn to shit on Saturday."

"I know," Rich said sheepishly, "I just can't."

I have known Rich long enough to know he wasn't coming. He works hard and is good at what he does. We have been good friends for a long time. We know each other and we both knew how the conversation was going to go. One of us has their priorities all fucked up. Most of the world will say it's me. Rich must have given Paul my number because I got a text from him. Paul specializes in guiding on New York's Finger Lakes. The one he spends the most time on is Canandaigua Lake.

All during the rest of dinner, my mind was somewhere else. I would latch onto threads of the conversation but I was preoccupied. I kept moving between memories of past perch outings and wondering where on earth I had left my spin-fishing stuff?

Years ago, more than I want to count, I had my boat set up for trolling for spring salmon. It was very early in the spring. Too early, as we could not entice any salmon or trout. Steelhead and silver salmon always come before any other coldwater species. It was about noon and the sun was bright and the cold wind blew right through you. After five hours of nothing, it was becoming likely that more nothing would be the result for the day. Throwing in the towel was an unsavory option, the antithesis of "one more cast." My mind was frantic and whirling, the two older fishermen staring at me with a certain intensity. Showing up back at home on a sunny spring day could result in the "honeydew" jar's lid opening. The honeydew jar, as I was told, was a form of matrimonial manipulation. It seems that the wife would inventory all the odd jobs that needed doing. Then she would write them all down separately on little pieces of paper. She would then place all these little pieces of paper in a mason jar. Then she would put a very cute label, HONEYDEW, on the jar. It was a sarcastic play on the phrase "things for honey to do." During interruptions of marital bliss, when a husband for whatever reason let his guard down, he found himself drawing from the jar. I would eventually nickname the thing the *Honeyscrew* Jar.

So coming in early was a bad option. I told my fishing companions about an old story I had heard. It was from a real old timer. He would tell of outrageous catches of giant perch this time of the year. He would sit on the old Shadigee Pier and catch one after the next until his arms ached. The Shadigee Pier was long gone. I had never seen it. I did know that the foundations were still there. I cracked up the boat engine's lower unit the previous fall just to prove it. This many years later, I can close my eyes and recall the cooler just overflowing with giant perch. It had been a long time since I fished to harvest fish. In recent times, I have become a proponent of catch-and-release. I do occasionally keep a few fish, but it has been a very long time since I harvested a big batch of fish.

Leaving the restaurant for home had me deep in thought—trying very hard to recall where I stored all my spin-casting equipment. When I was young, spin fishing was relatively new. It had taken the fishing world by storm. Coupled with the vastly improved monofilament fishing line, my eight-year-old brain in its fresh wisdom declared this type of fishing the forever method. I spent the next several years becoming the greatest spin fisherman in the world. I would be in the backyard daily placing Roostertails and Rapalas and Rattletraps into milk cartons and ashtrays and ultimately baby-food jars. My proficiency would later be rewarded with a self-created obsolescence. I would find and fall in love with fly fishing so deeply as to honestly call it one of the great loves in my life. Pragmatism would have me store away my spinning gear. I know some guys who try to fly fish for some deep-dwelling species. But fly fishing is really a surface or near-surface sport. I have seen flyfishermen who would never hold any other fishing tackle—this is the depth of the commitment to fly fishing—and with lots of lead sinkers, fish deep for walleyes in the heat of the summer. I guess every compulsion has its dumb fucks.

I tend to be anal. Yeah, I know it. This forces me to put up my sporting gear in such a way that some of it has lasted a very long time. I have a corner in my basement with rod racks and big Tupperware boxes and a large cabinet that houses most of my spin-fishing stuff. My old boss, the comedian George Carlin, used to do a routine about stuff. How your house is just a place for your stuff. When you ran out of room for your stuff, you needed a bigger place. That other people's stuff is shit and that your shit is stuff. I always felt this applied more so to outdoorsmen than to any other group.

As I was rummaging through the old stuff while looking for my spin-fishing gear, nostalgia started to creep in. You have to be so careful of nostalgia. It is one of the strangest and potentially dangerous functions that the human brain can perform. Faulkner once said, "Memory believes before knowing remembers." Nostalgia is a mechanism by which our brain "Photoshops" our memories before tossing them into the long-term memory bin. That part alone can be tricky. The real dangerous part is that every so often a memory is recalled and further "Photoshopped," or selectively improved.

I finally found the area in my basement that had the gear I wanted. I picked a seven-foot, one-piece G. Loomis spinning rod. Its one-piece design made it very sensitive. I also picked an eighties vintage Shimano spinning reel, the kind with all the ball bearings. It was made during a time when men believed that the more blades a razor had, and similarly the more bearings a reel had, the better. The rod-and-reel outfit worked well together. I opened the drawer that was labeled monofilament. I had forgotten just how much line I had. Dozens of boxes and miles of line. I picked out a premium six-pound test. Would it still be good? I kept it out of direct light, or any light at all—it was stored in a cool dark place. Perfect storage conditions.

As I put the line on the spinning reel's spool, this all felt familiar in a distant way. I tied on a small jig and put several more in an old Plano tacklebox. I added a pair of needle-nose pliers, some swivels, and sinkers. The sinkers made me laugh: They were made of the dreaded substance—lead. I recalled how effective lead was to use and how bad it was for everything else in the environment. The last item I rummaged was an old Coleman cooler. It was the kind everyone had, once upon a time. It was metal painted a familiar Coleman green, and it sported a built-in bottle opener—clearly meant for the uncapping of beer. I was shuffling around in a time warp, when two of the main ingredients of outdoors recreation were lead and beer.

I loaded up my car; I was going to meet Paul at eight that morning. I knew the drive to the lake pretty well. I timed it so I could get some ice and snack at a convenient mart along the way. Canandaigua is a beautiful lake, typical of the Finger Lakes. They were formed by glacial activity and are the home of the great Iroquois Nation. Some of the lakes even still had names given by the tribes. The name Canandaigua is derived from the Seneca name *Ga-nun-da-gwa*, which translates to "the chosen spot." The lake has become a summer spot for the affluent in the Rochester, New York, area. The lake is crowded from Memorial day to Labor Day, weekends being so full that by the peak during the Fourth of July, you can walk across the lake going from boat to boat. Then, after Labor Day, as if someone flipped a switch, it becomes eerily empty.

I pulled into the boat launch a bit early. A few boats were there, and I helped a pair of old fishing buddies launch theirs. It was typical boat-launch behavior: help and pump. Pumping them in a friendly way for any helpful information they might offer. They told me they were out yesterday and could not find any fish. Paul pulled in the parking lot right on time. We launched his boat. He had a similar story of difficulty finding fish in days prior. Perch start to yard up in the fall, smaller schools merging into bigger schools. This takes place until finally they start their spawning frenzy very early in the spring.

As we worked our way out into the lake, very dark and threatening skies brightened: Indian Summer would hang on for one more day. It even began to heat up enough that I stripped layers until I was down to a T-shirt. The fishing started off slow and difficult. It was just fine because the sun on my face was recharging me. We were fishing with "mousies," small minnows that perch seem to love. The Loomis outfit was the right choice. I could feel the subtlest of takes. Looking around, several other perch guys were the only ones fishing. The houses and cottages ringing the lake were dark. It had a post-apocalyptic feel; spooky in a way, but comforting in another. If the ghosts of the Seneca were here, they now reveled in solitude. While fishing Paul and I talked. We agreed that the best strategy was to keep moving until we found the fish.

In my youth, there were no limits on panfish. Men would take copious amounts. Today, New York State has a limit of fifty perch per person. Paul said he would give me his fish. Eventually we did find the fish. There were times when they were hot and heavy. Minute by minute, we added them to the cooler. That big, old cooler was filling up.

"Where do you suppose we are in terms of the limit?" I asked Paul.

"I'm not sure," he said. "We started out so slow."

I looked at him and he looked at me. I was thinking that this seemed like just the thing that falls under guiding "duties." I started to laugh, and being a bright guy, he picked up on it. It would be cruel not to help after laughing. In moments, we determined that sixteen more fish would end the day. In a short while we were done and heading back to the boat ramp.

It was mid-afternoon and I had my ice chest full of fall-summer treasure. I didn't know weeks before what bounty the witches of November would allow me. It was a throwback pleasure and I was deeply pleased. Lifting the cooler out of the boat caused me to remark how heavy a hundred perch could be. I helped Paul at the boat launch but decided to fight the urge to dally. I had one hundred fish to fillet. In my head I calculated that if I kept things moving I could pull off a fresh fish fry that evening. I kept thinking "Isn't Indian Summer something!"

I got home and I did fillet one hundred yellow perch. Some were an honest sixteen inches. The favorite fish of family and friends is the walleye. The yellow perch, being a close cousin of the walleye, is a close second. With my hands nicked and scraped and cut up from sharp gill plates and slight nicks from a razor sharp knife, I began to cook the old-fashioned fry. Thin-sliced chips and onions, fillets dipped in milk and then dredged in simple flour with garlic salt and white pepper. It was heavenly.

I called my mother, and my wife called a friend, offering up some of the Indian Summer bounty. It seems like the news went out over a wire. Shortly after, the phone began to ring with "inquiries." People were excited about the news of the catch. A few perch here and a few there, and it wasn't long before the bounty was gone. I had mixed feelings. Fish never taste better than when it's just caught. Once frozen, it's still good—but compared to fresh, it's a distant second. I was chatting with an aunt who had come for her share. I asked. "Why do you think everyone came out of the woodwork for the fish?"

She replied, "It reminded me of the old days. When your grandfather would come home from a trip. He would call everyone and divvy up the catch."

It was all about a time from the past. Food sharing is so basic. The act was the root of every clan and village. The calls I received over the next several days were filled with thanks and stories.

Woods

I am as free as nature first made man,
Ere the base laws of servitude began,
When wild in the woods the noble savage ran.
                                    —*John Dryden*

W hen we mention "the woods," the images that come through
are of wild places with a certain promise of pristine—of the planet
Earth in a virginal state. As a young boy in school, I was made to
memorize certain poetical works. I'm sure almost everyone has
some recollection of one of my favorites: "I went to the woods
because I wished to live deliberately, to front only the essential
facts of life, and see if I could not learn what it had to teach, and
not, when I came to die, discover that I had not lived." That is
Henry David Thoreau, in one sentence, a long sentence, emoting
the power of nature on our nature. Of course on the other end
of the poetry spectrum is Joyce Kilmer's much maligned work
"Trees," whose opening stanza blights memories the world over:

I think that I should never see
A poem as lovely as a tree.

Not very good but to each their own taste. Of course, if you can't see the forest for the trees, then you may need some time in the woods. While there, you may ponder the age-old question: "If a tree falls in the forest and no one is around to hear it, does it make a sound?" There is a difference between a forest and a wood. Originally, forest meant a royal hunting ground. Along that line of thinking, the forest is often thought of as large and diversified. Woods, on the other hand, are often thought of as pedestrian and accessible. It is really about seeing the forest for the trees.

As humans, the woods hold a duality. On some levels, they present a metaphor about the place from which we came. Wild men living in the woods. For epochs in time, we wanted to escape the woods, to build a civilization and escape the oppression of a hard life with challenges at the core of simple survival. In response, we built villages, towns, and cities. In that departure from survival, we found we left important parts of ourselves back in the woods. Our humanity, the very thing that makes us who we are, was left behind. This is the part of us that someone working in a cubicle on the twenty-first floor of a building in the financial district in Manhattan has a hard time feeling. Ironically, some of the most expensive housing is adjacent to Central Park. In most cases this is a sincere attempt to feel the woods.

When A.A. Milne wrote a story of a young boy whose life was most complete while in his hundred-acre woods with his friends, it touched a nerve. The adventures of Winnie the Pooh, frolicking with other creatures in the woods, offered a sense of belonging and well-being. Theodore Roosevelt understood the importance of wild and natural places. He created the national park system to protect wild places. Mostly those efforts were duplicated at the state and local levels. As a result, some woods were protected so that we could reconnect with our humanity, if only on a limited basis, to gain a sense of perspective.

I am one of those souls who feels the call. I need to unplug from the electronic world and reconnect with my own humanity.

The question is always how and where. As a young boy, I was part of the great American indoctrination. As children we were taught to memorize things that were symbolic of the American dream. I remember as part of a second-grade pageant memorizing and singing Woody Guthrie's "This Land is Your Land." Ironically, we sang the first several verses and never got to the subversive lyrics that illuminated Woody's leftist views.

In the end the song was sanitized and the political verses were removed when the song was recorded. The resulting song made a large sum of money, presenting a quandary for its author. Meanwhile, in mainstream America, in a second-grade pageant, I believed that this land was made for you and me. The seed that was planted then grew as I became a man with a yearning for that land. In those days we had some rigid ideas of where the woods were. They were either out West in the places loved by John Muir or the far north from Canada to Alaska. People flocked to these places in mind-numbing numbers. The approximate number of visitors to Yellowstone National Park from March 1, 1872, until December 31, 2014, was 166,845,437. I know that covers more than a century but the average in the last twenty years is over three million per year. About half that many go to Alaska. That's a lot of footprints *not* to leave.

In the 1980s, people started to enjoy a business boom. It allowed many to do the expensive things they always wanted to do. Places and things that were once only available to the rich came within reach to almost all. For fly fishers, the world was our oyster. We could insert ourselves into all those snazzy magazine-cover places. At first, it was nirvana. The promise of the wonderful woods was kept. It was immaculate and inexhaustible. Lodges opened all over the northern woods. Floatplanes ferried customers at a breakneck pace. Thirty-inch-plus trout ate mouse patterns. The wealth seemed unlimited.

Eventually the unthinkable happened. Paradise was spiraling away. Conspicuous consumption placed its gross obese weight upon a fragile ecosystem and it was being ruined. Those sports from the East saw familiar patterns. The notion that any place was bulletproof fell away in a tragic awakening. All those wading boots trampling redds, beads and hooks tearing away mandibles, sloppy septic conditions, all coming in a relentless tide proved that no ecosystem was immune, no matter how immense.

I remember my last trip to Alaska. I felt like I was part of an immoral assault on Mother Earth. That was some time ago. I have in recent times thought about going back. It has been the last two presidents now that have told us things are getting better, but they are not. The downturn has forced many lodges out of business. In a way, it was a big self-correction. The waves have lessened. As the ecology has proven time and again, if given a chance, nature can come back. This is not the first time this has happened. Humans as slow learners allow history to repeat itself. Many years ago, perhaps the beginning of last century, saw a culture of the woods. The Northeast sport camps sprung up. It was an important part of Americana. In the states of Vermont, New Hampshire, and Maine a camp often consisted of a main lodge house, several guest cabins, and staff cabins usually situated upon the shore of a fishy body of water. The sport camps obviously had fishing but also accommodated hunting. Bear, moose, deer, grouse, and caribou were all fair game. (The last caribou in the United States was shot by Cornelia T. Crosby, otherwise known as Fly Rod Crosby. She was a well-known huntress and friend of renowned shootist Annie Oakley.)

Any of the local historians in the Northeast can provide old black-and-white photos of sports and copious amounts of game. Men and women with giant salmon and brook trout nailed to a board by the hundreds. Money shots of game poles with giant game hanging in large numbers. In my case, it is hard to look at some of these photos. I am sure that the outdoorsmen of the era felt the same way we did about the North and the West—that it was just so plentiful, the resource would always be there. If you look at the photos you can see no malice in any face. It was all pleasure to have had their time in the woods. In the end, the whole enterprise collapsed. The sport camps that were the way so many sports in the East found their way into the woods struggled to hang on. In the end most faded while the rest found ways to stay. In every case some sort of rehabilitation was effected. The camps and the people who tied their lives to them fought for conservation. Today a rare commodity exists in the Northeast of America. The grand old camps thrive in a similar fashion to days gone by. The game under good stewardship is again breathtaking.

I have been going to my favorite woods for about a decade. I have fallen in love with those old camps. That place is called the "North Woods" in Northern Maine. It encompasses more than 3.5 million acres and 155 unincorporated townships. Within these boundaries resides both the Saint John and Allagash Rivers. You will also find numerous lakes, ponds, streams, creeks, and cricks. (If you don't know the difference between a creek and a crick then you need to read *How to Fish a Crick* by Patrick F. McManus.) You will find a fine forest with balsam firs, black spruce, northern white cedars, white spruce, yellow birch, paper birch, quaking aspens, Eastern white pines, speckled alders, Eastern hemlocks, white-tailed deer, moose, black bears, bobcats, coyotes, red foxes, fisher cats, otters, mink, martens, weasels, beavers, porcupines, muskrats, red squirrels, snowshoe hare, olive-sided flycatchers, white-throated sparrows, wood ducks, common yellow-throats, American robins, great northern loons, ruffed grouse, spruce grouse, blackflies, mosquitos, deerflies, midges, numerous and great hatches including giant—I mean big motherfucking, more than three inches long, day-glow greenish-yellow, dream-disturb-ing—Green Drakes, blueback trout, landlocked Salmon, togue (lake trout). And last, but certainly not least, the Eastern brook trout. I know I have missed some residents like the lynx and bald eagle. There is also Furbish's lousewort. It is an endangered plant that lives only in the Saint Johns Valley. In the early 1970s, there was a project to dam the upper Saint Johns, it was about a $227 million-dollar hydro-electric project. That is a whopper of a project in 1970s currency. This pretty little plant was thought to be extinct. Then in 1976, a man named C. D. Richards, whose job it was to conduct an environmental impact study before any work could begin, rediscovered the plant named after Maine artist Kate Furbish.

The part I love, aside from derailing the project, is that Furbish's lousewort is considered a Lazarus Taxon. (Because it was rediscovered.) Even more fun is the fact that there is an Elvis Taxon and a Zombie Taxon. All this came about in the early seventies, so you have to figure this is a confluence of science and the drug culture.

Late last fall, I commissioned a bamboo fly rod especially for fishing the North Woods. I didn't really have it commissioned, I had it made by my friend Jim Mills. (I don't have enough money to commission anything.) It is a seven and a half foot, 4-weight, based on a Paul Young perfectionist taper. It is flamed its entire length and the hardware is wrapped in orange and black thread. The reel seat is a high-polished silver with a burled maple insert. I had the end cap set with a large green tiger's eye by a jeweler friend of mine. I ended up matching it with a fine Peerless 1A reel. When I hold it in my hands, I just well up with all kinds of emotion. It goes from pride of ownership to awe of the craftsmanship. Really the only thing missing is its equal in nature: the Eastern brook trout attached by a fine tapered leader.

I have made it a tradition to spend a week in the spring and a week in the fall at the Bradford Camps on Munsungan Lake. I have this weakness to troll pretty tandem flies for landlocked salmon. Munsungan lends itself to this perfectly. The current issue was that I had this pretty little rod that needed to connect with pretty brook trout. If a bamboo fly rod ever had a calling, this was it. Beneath all this rationalization was the simple greed, plain avarice than manifested itself in expanding my time in the North Woods. Also in the maelstrom of *want* was the desire to find and experience more sport camps in "my" woods.

In reading the stories of those camps and the glory that those sports basked in yesteryear, what was once common is now rare, yet the possibility has hung on and preserved that way of communion in the woods, so it could be done in a way comparable if not better than the heyday of yesteryear. My search had me beginning a correspondence with a nice man named Jason Bouchard. He is the owner of an old sporting camp called Chandler Lake Camps. The place had a lengthy history. The camps are situated under the pleasant gaze of the Chandler Mountain range in historic Aroostook County. Starting in 1902, the camp boasted extraordinary hunting for trophy deer and moose. It also had a riches of ruffed grouse and wild brook trout. The place, like some of the others in that area, is like stepping out of a time machine. The conversations with Jason revealed that I am a dry-fly junkie with an unnatural penchant for Green Drake hatches. Not very original, but heartfelt to my core. At some point Jason felt my maniacal yearnings and the conversations started to include discussion of a recent addition to Chandler Lake Camps.

The recent addition was a place called the 4th Musquacook Lodge. The lodge is situated on, obviously, 4th Musquacook Lake. I was told that we could book the whole lodge for ourselves and our families. I was fishing with my father and his wife, my wife Mae, and my almost one-year-old son, Jerry. Jason kept telling me of these amazing Green Drake hatches. His recounting went on to tell of the big brook trout that were feasting on the bugs. In a lifetime of hunting and fishing, I have learned to take things with a grain of salt. I have been screwed more times than a two-dollar French whore. Most recently this past fall. I booked a whitetail bow hunt with an outfit that claimed they had the best whitetail hunting in America's "heartland." They were situated in the legendary Pike County. A few conversations later I was being frequently warned that this was trophy hunting and it was not uncommon *not* to see deer. It was big deer, not numbers of them. The hunt was approaching, and I had come down with a flu I nicknamed the "death march flu." I called the owner to try and move my hunt. He told me that this was the Super Bowl of whitetail deer hunting and if I miss it I was "shit out of luck." On the bright side, I was informed that I was lucky to have been able to book a hunt with him and his famous/infamous lodge. It's prison love like that that keeps me leery.

Jason was nothing but a gentleman on the phone and his lodge at Chandler had a good reputation. I have learned that this is a lot like dating—you can either become celibate or buy one of those inflatable donuts to sit on until you get over the last pounding. I booked the trip to 4th Musquacook.

The plan was to spend a week at Bradford Camps and then go directly to Chandler Lake Camp on 4th Musquacook. In past years, we always hired a floatplane to take us from our place in Grand Lake Stream into the North Woods. This trip, because we were going to multiple places, we decided to drive. I was actually looking forward to it. It is about three hours from our place. We drove north until we got to Ashland. It is a short ride from Ashland to the six-mile gate. I don't know what it is about gates, but they always give me a good feeling. Some delineation from the outside world. I feel that way about the gates in Yellowstone and I feel that way about the North Woods, too. Beyond this point, you leave the outside world behind. Symbolically it works. The gate in the North Woods is an amazing thing. You stop and pay to enter. The fee is variable and factors things like age and residency. The fees are taken by a nonprofit that maintains the logging roads. More importantly, they allow for access in the entire woods. Considering all the logistical issues with various and changing land owners and the remoteness of the whole thing, it is miraculous. There was a time when you had to deal with all kinds of gates. Some were open, some were fee-based, and some were simply closed. This open access is amazing. What is not amazing is the roads themselves. You need a stout truck with even more stout tires. Someday I am going to write a book of things I have regretted. It will be filled with tales of ex-wives, dealing with the US government, leaving teenage children home without supervision, and driving a four-door sedan to Bradford Camps. I am told that someday I will laugh about it. That may very well be, but it's going to take a while for *me* to laugh.

I go to Bradford because I love to troll tandem flies. It is an old method and works well for landlocked salmon. Trolling is not something I want to do all the time, but the ten or so days a year I do is about right. My time there this year was a bit difficult. No matter how nice the camp or how conscientious the people, weather calls the shots. My strategy on Munsungan has always been to troll until I catch a hatch. I have had some amazing hatches there, but you have to be patient. That lake, Munsungan, can be a moody bitch. The first four days the wind was a tormenting one, to the point where boat control was difficult. There is a term called a "salmon chop" that implies a small steady chop is good for the fishing. My experience is that is true up to a certain point. When a salmon chop becomes a surf chop, the fishing stinks. The last day started like the rest—a windy affair. The evening after dinner saw the wind lay down and the lake start to lay down, as well. I decided to take my wife and give our son his first boat ride. I set the lines out and after a while, Mae commented, "Did you see all the little fish heads that keep popping out of the water?" I did see them. Some kind of blue-winged olive was coming off. I needed to go back to the cabin and retrieve my beautiful bamboo rod.

Yes, I had left the rod in my cabin. I had kept it in the boat all week and started to feel that it was jinxing me. I have tried not to be a superstitious fly fisher, but why should I be the only one? I don't troll bamboo, it takes almost no time at all to impart memory in the tip, caused by dragging the heavy fly line. Soon, I had the evening planned just right. I put on a nicely-tied blue-winged olive pattern in size 8. A school of salmon was all around me. The salmon I had caught trolling seemed smallish this year. There was some mention of a heavier-than-usual togue popula-tion. The rising fish seemed larger. The first cast brought a jarring strike. Minutes later an aggressive fifteen-inch salmon came to the net. The first fish ever caught on my squaretail special fly rod was a salmon! It was not how I imagined it, but it was so good. The action on the rod was sweet and she handled the ruffian with a deftness that only comes from bamboo. I would follow that school of salmon until well past dark. I am not sure how many I caught. Plenty. How many is a plenty? More than twenty but less than fifty. When I got to the dark, it was pitch black. Like a home-run hitter breaking out of a slump, I was due, and it felt good. The next morning, we would continue on in the North Woods.

We flew into camp on 4th Musquacook. What hit me immediately was the fact that the buildings were not the old dark peeled logs I was expecting. The logs were lighter, which indicated a newer lodge. In getting a deeper understanding of the place, I learned it was built in 1969 by executives at International Paper. It was their VIP playground in which they had fun with initials like IPVIP. Fucking morons. These were the guys that raped the woods with their clear-cutting and profit at all cost. In a wildly inappropriate stroke of unfortunate irony, they set up their outdoor paradise in a pristine bubble they saved for themselves and clients they needed to woo to get into their pants monetarily. One of the good things in life is that the worm almost always turns. International Paper underwent an intense restructuring that saw them sell off millions of acres of land. Part of this sell off included the VIP fishing lodge that stood before me. In a way it sparked a thrill, it almost felt like I was poaching the king's trout. I have always had a certain contempt for the corporate aristocracy. At one time sneaking onto elite golf courses with a fly rod in my golf bag was the thrill ride. There are some hogs (usually) swimming in a lot of the ponds on the back nine. Standing in front of a judge in your twenties buys you some slack as it is attributed to indiscretion of youth. Standing in front of the same judge in your thirties will get you a look of annoyance. In your forties your attorney is trying to negotiate a fine and keep the community service to a minimum, not to mention tap dancing to avoid several weekends in the clink. Now that I am in my fifties, it has been a long time since I felt that feeling of my trespassing self. I would never trespass onto a property where the owner was a hardworking, tax-paying guy. Big rich country clubs and giant corporate retreats are something else—even though I was here totally legit, violating the old corporate vibe was still a thrill.

Musquacook is Abenaki for "Where the white birch grows." In researching the Abanaki peoples, all you really find is a piecemeal history fraught with sorrow. The Abenaki were part of the Wabanaki confederacy who were bitter adversaries of the Iroquois. The member tribes of the Wabanaki confederacy shared a root language. They all spoke a derivative of the Algonquian tongue. The term Algonquian means "the peoples of the east." The people of the east suffered the "great dying." During the period of the 1500s and 1600s, European disease caused the death of more than seventy-five present of the Native Americans in New England. To cope with the tragedy, the Abenaki strategy was to merge after periods of heavy losses and move north and hide their existence from more powerful enemies around them. This fugue of attrition and regrouping has made it hard to know them and their history. In the North Woods, their legacy is the names they left behind. Like the name Musquacook—"where the white birch grows." I like that the name contains a verb like "grows." The language emotes a certain optimism. I often wonder what would have happened if the Native Americans were the ones with the super bugs and heightened immune systems. The world would surely have turned out so different.

That first night had me arriving at Musquacook ahead of the rest of our party. They would follow the next morning. As the floatplane landed at the dock, the entire lodge staff greeted me. Jason was there along with his lovely partner Sherry Morris. Fill-in guide, Brian Donaguy, and fireplace heat retainers Sage and Parker (very birdy English setters). I was shown where I was staying upstairs in the lodge. Coming through the front door set the tone of the place. There was a great room with a dining table and an oversize fireplace. Though the day was gray and damp and chilled, the fireplace was warm, crisp, and cheery. My room was spacious with electricity and internet. I know that I mentioned being unplugged but there was also a nice feel about being able to take down, at a relaxed pace, the mountain of emails that had accumulated the prior week at Munsungan (which is unplugged). The lodge itself was situated on a point that allowed for lovely views in all directions. Down at the lake was a shallow inlet that had constant moose traffic. In another direction was a field full of lupine and some almost-red flowers. My favorite part of the lodge was the screened-in porch. It allowed a view of the scenic surroundings with a nice glass of Scotch (Oban for this trip) and a fine cigar (my father's cigar this trip) without being bled by black flies, deer flies, and mosquitos.

It did not take long to get my things put up. In a moment Jason asked, "Do you want to go fishing?" Shortly thereafter we were in the truck going down a woods road. In a while, we had pulled up to the trailhead. We would hike into Chantilly Pond. The rain during the previous week meant that the hike would be muddy and difficult. The soft and slippery mud with the hard and twisted tree roots meant caution was important. With some care we emerged out of the dark woods at the edge of the pond. The place was alive with activity. The pond seemed at least forty acres. It may have been even larger as we never reached the back half. We could never get past all the fish in the front half. Standing on the shore, it was easy to see a major Green Drake hatch coming off and *Salvelinus fontinalis* feasting all over the place. The sight of all this had me stringing up the squaretail special as quickly as it had Jason finding and setting up the canoe he had stashed there.

Being an honest-to-goodness *Ephemera guttulata* aficionado, I had always set the benchmark at a trip I took to northern Labrador about fifteen years ago. Up until this point, the Green Drake hatch I had there while staying at the legendary Minipi Lodge was king. They were big bugs with deep, dark-green bodies. The hatch covered a large area and giant brook trout were slurping them down. That benchmark now was toppled. The Drakes coming off Chantilly Pond were the biggest I had ever seen. As I watched one monster emerge I could hear a faint *pop*. I heard the hatch! After so many years in the entertainment business, and all those same years working in front of big sound systems, my hearing has taken a hit. Even so, I could *hear* these bugs coming off. I did manage to catch a freshly emerged fly. It measured a hair over three inches. What the hell am I supposed to do with that? And, they were so bright. It was a day-glow greenish yellow. Most importantly, the trout were loving them. Jason had tied on my line a large fly with a grey body and pink wings. Of course it was the last one of those he had, which meant it instantly got chewed beyond recognition.

That first night on Chantilly Pond, we landed more than twenty-five brook trout. They were all 14–20 inches. The last fish of the night was so beautiful. That, along with the special rod, the pretty sunset, the nice shot of Oban, and the perfect taste of a fine rolled cigar, made my heart ache. That last fish was a male a bit anxious for the fall. He was already sporting a large hump on his back and a deep kype in his jaw. Beyond that, he had the deep greens with bright spots of blue and red. The orange on the fins and belly was so deep and vibrant they were beyond what you'd see in a Crayola box. This night, the contrasts were far apart. Here in the net was as beautiful a brook trout I had ever seen, and he was attached to my fine bamboo rod with a big dry fly hanging from its mouth. This was the mountain top, the true holy grail of fly fishing. Though there was fishing light left, nothing could be made better. The trout was released, I broke down the rod, and just enjoyed the pretty of the rest of the sunset. I was smitten with this pond and hoped we would fish her again. I found sleep easily that night and for the first time in a long time, I dreamt about fishing.

The next morning, I began to notice a culinary pattern. It seemed that the cook, a woman who a short time before had made her living hauling lumber in one of those monster trucks seen on the backroads, was actually a chef. The food that Chef Sherry prepared was easily the finest I had ever experienced in any outdoor camp. (That, I must tell you, is very high praise as I had come from Chetola Resort in North Carolina just ten days earlier; that property had a wonderful four-star restaurant called Timberlake's.) Luckily, we never had a rigid mealtime. That would have been nervous-breakdown territory. The real crisis was one of girth. How does one resist the sound of a blow torch in the kitchen and the smell of caramelizing crème brûlée? It is impossible. All you can do is starve yourself somewhere down the line. The good news was you never had to choose between fishing time and eating time, they would hold dinner if you needed it. Every day as you went out the door to fish, there was an inquiry about what to have for dinner. Crazy.

After breakfast, we were on our way to Manassas Pond. It was similar to the prior evening in that you drove for a bit and then took the trailhead down to the pond. Good boots were a boon for these woods. I think the right footwear is critical for any stay in the woods. If you screw up your feet or take a nasty spill, the trip can be compromised. The trail in was a little better than the previous day's. Drying had occurred. Down at the pond, the ritual was similar to the previous day. I strung up the rod while Jason made ready the canoe. The Drake hatch that we had the night before comes off on several of the area ponds but at slightly different times. We were here to see if it was on at this place yet. Weather was wonky on this day, as it really had been since I had come to Maine. The wind just would not exit the natural stage. This day brought different fishing than the previous evening. Somewhere during the mid-morning, my father and Brian had showed up. There was a blue-winged olive hatch going and some sort of very light, between straw and white, Hendrickson-type hatch. To be honest, I had never seen it before. I recognize hatch types and try to possess flies accordingly. At the lunch spot we discussed the evening plans. I really wanted to share stories about the hatch I had encountered the evening before. I wanted my father to see those giant Drakes. It was decided that we would fish Chantilly again that evening.

The fishing on Manassas Pond was good. I had managed to catch nearly a dozen fish in the 14–18-inch range. Each brookie was as pretty as the next. I was using the Squaretail Special and the karma of the trip was beginning to set. You could see, once the Drake hatch started on this pond, it would catch fire (in a fly-fishing sense). The day was, by any account, hardcore fishing. The weather was again exerting her dominance. As I was breaking down my rod, I was looking forward to dinner. I was also offering a silent prayer for a calm night on Chantilly Pond. I also had made my heart thankful for the day's fish. These were very fat brookies with several weighing in at least two pounds. I was feeling high.

The dinner was spectacular. Even so, I was anxious to get my father onto Chantilly Pond. When you tell people about giant

Green Drakes hatching in large numbers like I was talking, people figure that in your exuberance the truth is taking a beating. Truth in fly fishing is a tough thing to get your head around. Really, any truth is a rare commodity. I knew my father would have to see for himself that these were not your run-of-the-mill size-6 Drakes.

The other part of the story is a bit more complex and emotional. There is this pond that my father pines for. He has fished it yearly religiously. The pond is fertile, and he usually catches lots of twelve-inch trout with a few biggies mixed in. Several days earlier he flew into "his" pond. He acquired it honestly. He went to her faithfully and loved her honestly. It is the emoting in these ways that give us title to certain waters. In his day on his pond, he had caught several very small trout. In a tragedy that harsh winters can deliver, my father's pond suffered a winter kill. He was downhearted about the affair and it was my hope that seeing what I had experienced the night before might provide some comfort. Nothing was going to remove the sting of the loss completely.

On the ride to the pond, we discussed the winter-kill fish. It turned out that Jason knew that pond well. Jason was able to tell us that my father's pond was prone to a kill every ten to fifteen years. There is some comfort in this knowledge. Like letting the fires burn in national parks, it is part of that pond's cycle. As fertile as this pond is, a growth rate for the fish of three to five inches a year was very possible. Though the fishery would not come back tomorrow, it would in a season or two. In a way that nature has of applying balance and harmony, there is a good chance that my father's pond will have a few "hot" years before it levels out and ultimately repeats the cycle of life.

The discussion about the winter kill helped the ride go quicker. We got out of the truck and onto that hard trail walk to the pond. We had had some rain during the day, which called for even greater caution. As we arrived on the shore of the pond, I could see my father's eyes surveying the scene. The Drakes were there, and fish were taking them as close as several feet from shore. A sense of anticipation was shared by all. It was a silent few moments until the rods were strung and the canoes were made ready. I fished with Jason and my father fished with Brian. It was not long until I could see his rod bowed with a heavy fish. I love to watch my father fish. He has a casting style that is just poetic. Brook trout are the most poetic of all fishes. Something about that makes me feel good. Though it did not cure the hurt about his pond, I could feel it draw some of it away.

I had one of those evenings that I dream of. It is the gift the fish gods give you perhaps once a decade or even two. The Squaretail Special got the full workout. It revealed the depth of its action. In the action, I could see and feel the genius of Paul Young. I would catch many heavy fish on this night. The hatch was even more perfect as the wind finally surrendered and fell away. The surface of the pond was like a mirror. Like a large dark pupil. They say that the eyes are the mirror to the soul. I was looking into the soul of the Mother Earth. The fish I caught would exceed the previous night in every way.

In life we pursue greatness in the endeavors we choose. In these things we hope for a brief glimpse of perfection. We try in earnest to obtain our "Opus." Some argue that you can only have one opus, and some argue that is not true. I don't really know how to define it. I do know it when it happens. We were landing heavy fish. Anything under 15 inches was rare. I was throwing a large Drake imitation. I just love the way bamboo lilts big dries upon the water. It is almost as if the fly tier imparts a little magic into the fly. That when the fly is cast, time slows ever so slightly, and for the briefest of moments the fly feels life. It lands upon the water of its own will.

The sun was angling lower and the distant clouds were glowing in pinks and purples. It was that time when light levels lower to the point where the odds turn in favor of the predators. In this world, Chantilly Pond, brook trout are the apex predators. In a pond this size, there are a handful that fear nothing. They have been cagey and have grown to a point where they rule the waters. In a cast, my fly takes the magic of the moment and makes the perfect landing. The ripples from the displacement push out concentrically. I watch intently. Poised and ready to strike back if the need arises. In a moment an eruption occurs. I set the hook and the rod bends toward the fish. This one is different from the other fish. There is a powerfulness that is moving up the line through the rod and into me. There is big substance to this fish. I can feel every shake of its head. The pull has taken the line out and now the fish is on the reel. The rod is a four-weight. This is a fight of finesse. Trying to muscle the fish could cause the light leader to break, or worse, the rod. In the first moments the outcome is unsure. Then the tide starts to turn. It will be about five minutes. The fish loses all its leverage as the net rises and the trout lays in the soft rubber of the net. I removed the fly and measured the fish. I am without words. I have a big lump in my throat. The beauty measured twenty-four inches and sported a deep belly. She was closer to four pounds than three. This was the fish of the trip. Truly the fish of almost two decades.

I didn't have much to say on the hike out. In the truck I found out that my father had had a good night. He was amazed at the heft of the Drakes. I took the ride in self-reflection. My emotions ran high. That this happened in "my" woods made it so much better. I didn't have to take an exotic journey.

When we returned to the lodge, I poured everyone a nice smooth glass of Scotch. The warmth of the alcohol spread across my body. Following the warmth came fatigue. I soon excused myself and crawled under several wool blankets. A deep sleep washed over me. I wish I could say that I was awash in some sort of revelation, but I wasn't. I can say that it was a deep restful sleep that led to a morning of satisfaction.

The morning broke with a steady blow causing whitecaps outside my window. I was wondering what the plan of the day would be. I can get into these moods if I have been fishing a long stretch of days in a row, where you just don't want to fuck around with poor conditions. At these times I dig down and rally together some fortitude and attitude. This was going to be one of those days. The weather, to spite me, continued to sour. Wind climbed, and rain fell, and my ire burned beneath a quiet and reserved exterior. I could tell that Jason was doing his best to try and figure it out. On days like these it must suck out loud to be a guide. To put together a game plan even when none made much sense. Then the announcement came that was like a sucker punch right in the stomach. We were to fish the Allagash River. I have fished that river several times and have done miserably. The river is fine, with a world-class reputation, but it withholds everything from me. I have been open-minded about the water but no more.

I was standing on the very rock I had stood on before. My father was literally thirty feet away and he was catching brook trout. I was fishing, and bright silvery, willing fallfish were the only things between me and getting skunked. This was my fourth time on the Allagash and the second time at this very spot. The few fallfish I managed to hook were a vast improvement from previous performances. In a fit of frustration, I handed the rod to Jason in hopes of learning something. What I learned is that there are waters that love us, places where we can do no wrong. It seems nature always provides a balance and she gives us places where we can do no right. The weather conditions worsened, and it was decided that we should go to the camp for lunch. My eyes immediately brightened. If there was a worthy consolation prize for stinking up the river, it was a homemade lunch by Sherry. An amazing fiddlehead soup and grilled cheese goes a long way to helping with a bad attitude. I got cleaned up and enjoyed a glass of scotch with a homemade brownie. Oddly enough they went together rather well. I didn't actually dunk the brownie in the single malt, but it did cross my mind.

After another wild dinner (you can actually get fat here—or in my case, fatter) Jason had a new pond that he wanted to try. He had guests coming after us who enjoy this pond quite a bit. Gin Pond sits a little higher up so the Drake hatch comes off a bit later. Jason really liked this pond and was anxious to show her off. Jason liked this pond quite a bit. She had super clear water and big brook trout. If Jason was anxious to get there so was I.

The weather improved as the evening wore on. It would never get to the point where it could be ignored. The ride to the trailhead was a bit more challenging. The hike into the pond was more challenging, too. I knew that if these ponds were a breeze (a wind metaphor) to get to, the fishing would be average. The difficulty of getting in provided the protection these waters needed. The greatest value of staying at a camp up here is they take the very difficult tasks and do most of the hard parts. You still have to keep your ass in the truck seat and hike the trail to the fish. I had done both of those things and was rewarded by the sight of one of the prettiest ponds I have ever seen. As I was stringing up my rod, I peeked over the shore at the water. The water was so very clear—I searched my recollections and could think of no water that was ever clearer. Standing there being held in place by the beauty of the perfection of creation. This was the kind of view Adam and Eve had before the apple incident. It struck me how rare places like this are and how important it is to protect them. The pond's name is not really Gin Clear Pond, in fact I've lied about all the names in this story. Well, not all the names, Jason Bouchard is a real name. It is fun to wax poetically but, that has to be close-ended, because, man, you have to fish. In the survey of the hatch, it seemed that the biggies, the giant Drakes, were very infrequent. It felt like they would need just a little more time. That was okay because there were a bunch of other bugs coming off. There were "regular" Drakes, around size 8; then there were some Blue-winged Olives, Hendricksons, and some that were like very light quills of a kind and nature new to me; there were other flies too. In the big picture, it was a lovely hodgepodge of choices that also gives a flyfisherman a very cool freedom. Like a good knuckleball pitcher, now you could throw junk. Having a counterculture soul and hating to always play by the rules, this was good for me.

The lake was so clear it was mind-boggling. Tying on bright "junk," the flies seemed to radiate a long way out. In fact, the extreme clarity allowed you to see trout coming from a long way away. Trying to hold steady with the sight of a large brook trout steaming toward your fly is really a test of patience and nerves. At one point I could see the white circle of an open maw for feet before it took my fly. She was a twenty-two-inch brook trout. She slid into the net as stunning as she was fat. That was the lasting impression of Gin Pond. Fat fish. That night saw about twenty big fish slide into the net. The following day was our last, and Gin Pond was where I wanted to spend it.

The day came, and the sun was shining and the wind seemed manageable. I was so damned excited on the way back to Gin Pond. I can't tell you why—a fisherman's instinct perhaps, but I just knew the place held some monsters. We had made arrangements to stay all day and fish until dark. Time was ticking away against my North Woods stay. I wanted to squeeze the last bit out of this last day. Mother Nature had other ideas. As we had the canoe readied, the wicked wind and charring sun came at us. We spent hours fighting off bad conditions. Later that evening, the wind acquiesced as the final remnants of sunlight slipped away. It allowed for perhaps a half-hour of good fishing. Hiking up the trail to the trailhead, I felt a sense of resigned frustration. I wondered when the real Drake Hatch would begin. I wondered if I could catch it better next year. I really wasn't complaining. How could I? I just had the best brook trout fishing in decades and perhaps ever. My Catholicism was kicking in with its version of guilt over greed. Like a child with a new toy, I just couldn't help it.

The following morning was even more cruel. The sun was shining on the fourth Musquacook. There was a serene flat calm broken every so many feet by rising fish. I stood on the porch with my lips pursed tightly. Fuck, I thought, fuck. Then a selfish thought crept into me. I could ask to stay an extra day. I knew Jason did not have any guests coming in over the next few days. I also knew he had wanted to get some fishing lessons from Sherry. The other obstacle was my wife. I had her in the North Woods for a long stay. I know she liked it and appreciated it —but I also knew that she had had enough. In relationships there has to be give and take. I always look at it like a big account we keep for each other. When you give, the account fills; when you take, it drains. I knew I was coming close to being overdrawn. I asked Jason if he was game. He was. To his credit, he loves what he does. I told him that I needed to see if it was okay with Mae.

Mae said yes with a smile. I knew it wasn't what she wanted, and my account was in arrears. I would have to fix that.

There it was—I had stolen a day! I don't get to do that very much. We have become a society that frowns upon stolen days. So much so that I invented a lie. My car, unexpectedly, would not be finished until the following day. I really wanted to say, "Fuck off, I needed an extra day in the North Woods, so I'm staying." We have become so politically correct. How is it that we have come to a point where we have to lie about how we feel? I tell people that I was born free, and if I died tomorrow, it wouldn't be free. One of the most tragic conversations I had recently was with a young man. He wanted to know what it was like to be free. I am not sure how it had come to this, but we live in a culture of deception. That is one of the reasons I crave the woods. Nature is brutally, refreshingly, lovely in her honesty. In a way she washes all the crap out of our souls. I despise that in an instant I get recovered in insincere shit. In a self-analytical moment, I understood the maneuvering for an extra day.

I was happy on the ride to the trailhead. I was happy stringing up my rod. I was happy to fish the first hour. Then like some running gag that just went too far, the weather got freaky. It did everything but snow. The wind howled out of the north, and then like a light switch being flipped, it howled out of the south. It drizzled, and it poured. About the time it poured, I decided to relax and enjoy the show. We took cover under some thick pines and waited out the rain. From the south, a large osprey came wheeling over the pond. Scouring with super eyesight, she locked onto a fish. Hundreds of feet were covered in seconds. The "twap" of the raptor hitting the water could be felt in my chest. Then with big heaving strokes, you could hear each labored wing beat, she lifted away with a nice brook trout dinner. In that moment, I envied her.

We struggled with the weather and the conditions until early evening. It was like our penance was finally paid. The air cooled and the wind died. The sun was lowering and glowering. Hatches started to come off. Over the next several hours, we managed to boat thirty-two trout. I also managed to miss enough big fish to haunt my dreams for a year. To say I never caught a monster would be a lie. The twenty-four-inch brook trout that I caught at Chantilly Pond was fat and heavy. That fish qualifies. I also know that I will keep coming back. That is the thing about fishing. If you give yourself to it, sooner or later you get your shot. The fish gods are extremely fair that way. It should be that way everywhere.

That is the difference between gods and men.

The Escape
(or,
Gone Missing and Presumed
to be Having a Good Time)

~~~~~~~~~~

The church and the whorehouse arrived in
the far west simultaneously. And each would
have been horrified to think it was a different
facet of the same thing. But surely they were
both intended to accomplish the same thing:
the singing, the devotion, the poetry of the
churches took a man out of his bleakness for
a time, and so did the brothels.
　　　　　　　　—*John Steinbeck, East of Eden*

There is a cliché that goes something like, "He who dies with
the most toys, wins." It is the mantra and ideology of people
who embrace the rat race and use it to keep other people down.
The quote was obviously thought up by a first-rate asshole, who
had perhaps only slightly more intelligence than the scores of

morons who quote it because it did take some twisted but creative thinking to make up.

I have a hard time with the rat race. I've never felt good about racing vermin. I understand that in most cases it's a necessary evil. We have obligations to other people who rely on us. So we punch clocks and work: the tying down of irreplaceable time at the expense of the human spirit. Within me, my human spirit deeply resents the theft of time in its linear fashion. I resent the rat race's toll on humanity. While I participate, marginally, my spirit is always looking over the fence. My brain daydreams about the prison break. To flee the rat race and to thumb my nose at Big Brother. The real issue becomes letting the people I love remain to founder. It is so easy to see people getting trapped. Credit card bills, utility bills, cable bills, high-speed internet bills, grocery bills, mobile-phone bills, redistribution of wealth bills (otherwise known as taxes), car bills, and the list goes on. We work to make money—mostly money that only pauses briefly in our own hands before being swept away to the folks who run the rats.

The ultimate handcuffing effect, the reason for getting caught up in the rat race (ironically), is the love we have for our family. It ties us to the rat race and in most cases keeps us in line. I do understand and I feel it too; I have this emotional understanding. But then I hear a voice on the wind telling me to escape. The longer I try to ignore the voice, the louder it becomes. It builds to a crescendo until I have no choice but to heed its call and run away from everything. All the while knowing that the rat race will still be here when I return, and will greedily accept me back and get its clutches on my soul. The escape is my short-term release valve.

The truth is, I am always looking for escapes, someplace I might run to. Lots of people do it. Mostly they call it planning a vacation. I sort of do it constantly. The older I get, the more I bolt. I have started to wonder if retirement is the completion of the process. If it is then, maybe, I am ready. The word retire indicates you were already tired once. I have always had a dubious sentiment toward being a cog in the wheel. I don't think I have gotten over the original tired. In an effort to be consistent I will just say that I am tired.

The latest escape had me eyeing a music event. I do have passions other than fly fishing. There was a concert at Red Rocks, outside of Denver. Red Rocks is an amazing place. It is a natural amphitheater designed by the gods, supplemented by man, and spiritually charged by cosmic forces that leave you in awe standing there within it. In the society of beatniks and hippies, it is a four-star destination in the guide to spiritually cool places.

I like to look at ticket-outlet websites on the computer. I saw a T-shirt I liked, which read, "I may be old but I got to see all the cool bands." Of course the implication is that the cool bands are all gone. However, a handful of old-timers are still rocking out. The Rolling Stones come to mind. Bob Dylan is no spring chicken. While perusing the survivors I came across Steely Dan, with a single front-row seat for a reasonable price. Sometimes single seats can be a bit tough to sell. I bought the ticket. After printing it out, I realized that Steve Winwood was the opening act. It felt good. I was committed to a trip to Colorado. The only thing that remained was finding a place to fish the week before the concert. It's always great when I can add fly fishing to my "other" passions.

The thought of fishing Colorado again really lit me up. Fly fishing the Rocky Mountains can be as good as it gets. The thought of fishing high alpine lakes and streams always makes me high. There is just something about wild Colorado trout—they seem to glow and effervesce. Holding a wild Cutthroat trout in all its glory spins you back in time. The fish is a true relic from Ice Ages past. They give you connections. Not only to pristine wilderness but also to pristine time. There is also something about

Colorado brown trout. The coloration ranges from butter to butternut squash and their sides are well-peppered with black and red spots. If you are very lucky, you will get the glowing green stripes down the back.

To do this running away from home correctly, it takes a while to get the knack. If it is done right, if you frame it correctly, it becomes a story, an adventure tailored to your own character. I think it is important to do that. To make magic from thoughts. It is really the utilization of sentience that allows us to star in our own adventures. It takes two things to get there: the first ingredient is imagination; the second is the self-discipline to follow through.

First, what needed doing was to find a place to fish before the concert. The concert was on a Monday, which was cool. I could book a regular block of fishing. These trips usually end on a Sunday and in this case, that would work out well. Getting ready to find a spot in Colorado had me all jazzed up. It was early in the season. The concert was on June 13. Fishing the week leading up to the concert would have me struggling to find clear water as the previous winter's snow would be at peak meltdown. It is problematic, but there was the other side of the coin. I would be early; the fish would be less pressured and therefore less jaded, if jaded at all.

I called one of the more famous fishing lodges in the Colorado Rockies. I was not surprised to find they were booked up. The woman was pleasant and tried to sell me a later trip. I explained that this was the week I needed to fish and could she recommend another lodge in Colorado. She went on to inform me that after "her" lodge, there was a big drop off in quality and that I would be far better off looking to Wyoming for quality fly fishing. The call ended shortly after that. I hung in the air for several moments, a bit shocked, and then a bit pissed. I remember thinking, "That *bitch!*" I have fished Colorado enough to know that the place is jammed with some of the finest trout water on the planet. In a way, it did motivate me to find that "lost" treasure I knew I could find if I put my nose to the ground.

I ended up calling the Broadacres Ranch in Creede, Colorado. I talked to a man name Bruce Tweeten. Bruce informed me that the ranch would not open until the following week and that run-off was streaming off the mountain peaks. After explaining about the show at Red Rocks and how I was trying to create a special fly for the trip and how I need to ditch the rat race, a pregnant pause followed. Bruce told me he would talk to the ranch owner and see if he could help make it happen.

A week later Bruce did call back. He told me he could do it, as long as I understood that the ranch would not be open yet. He said he would be my guide the whole time and that the customary gourmet food would not be there because the chef didn't arrive until they opened later.

I was thrilled.

"You know the water is still screaming in the Rio Grande?" Bruce said in a cautionary tone. His voice had that southwestern drawl that you hear in any good 1950s Western. I drew the connection to cowboy culture.

"I know I am a bit early but there are other waters around, right?" I asked. "Besides, I really wanted to do some high alpine fishing."

"We do have smaller waters on the ranch. We also have four nice lakes with wild fish in them," Bruce said. "I have been here for a while and they have never been stocked. They never get fished but if all else fails, we have them. We have some nice water high up, too."

I let him know that the trip was about more than catching fish. I didn't say that catching was *not* important. It pisses me off when I hear someone say something like, "We didn't catch any fish but that didn't matter, that's not what we go fishing for!"

Huh? If that is not what they go fishing for, then stay home. To catch fish is exactly what I go fishing for. Sometimes things get so bastardized that you lose sight of everything. I understand there are some damn fine intangibles and they do count, but I always try real hard to catch fish. I told Bruce, "Thank you very much." That I understood I was throwing the dice, but we would fish hard and it would work out. Bruce responded in his deep cowboy way: "Yup." I knew I was going to like him a lot.

I like making connections in life, to weave aspects of different parts of my life in a way that I can tie it all together in the end. In this specific event, my escape, I knew from the beginning that I wanted to create a fly for the trip. I had the name already. It would be called the "Deacon Blue-winged Olive." Here's where my idea of connecting comes in. You don't really have to know about the rock band Steely Dan except that one of their best songs, one of my favorite songs, one of the songs I was hoping to hear performed at Red Rocks, is called "Deacon Blues." Hence the fly called the Deacon Blue-winged Olive. The fly had to have some qualities that I could honestly relate to the song. It had to have a real jazz-blues vibe going. I think talking about trying to create this fly helped Bruce decide to open up the lodge to me a week early. I had a suspicion Bruce might have a tie-dyed cowboy hat hidden somewhere, if only in his distant past.

Anyone with any familiarity with me knows my fly-tying skills stink. I guess that gets right to the point. It also illuminates the fact that I was going to need help in the creation of the "new" fly. In thinking of who, my mind immediately seized on Carl Coleman. Carl owns a fly shop in my neck of the woods simply called Coleman's. Carl Coleman is one of the elder statesmen of Great Lakes tributary fly fishing. All those remarkable steelhead runs, football-size brown trout smashing Wooly Buggers, and various salmon haunting the tributaries of the Great Lakes looking for a fight were nonexistent before the 1960s. I know it seems funny, but when the Great Lakes were first stocked with salmonids, no one knew what to do. It is hard to believe, but countless fishermen drowned mostly because nobody knew how to take on the new fishery. On September 24, 1967, sixteen fishermen perished chasing silver salmon during a storm on Lake Michigan. A few years later, it happened again to fishermen in waders on Lake Erie. The late 1960s are filled with newspaper stories of fishermen finding glorious action in the once-barren Great Lakes, not paying attention to the weather, and then wishing they had. Big trout can have that effect. Carl was one of the pioneers on how to enjoy the sudden ichthyologic Elysium safely and successfully.

I walked into Coleman's and there was Carl, his usual ageless self. A tall, red-faced Englishman with pale blue eyes. We greeted each other and started catching up in a way only two old-time fly fisherman can. It is a mandatory but pleasant exercise. Then Carl asked, "What brings you to these parts?"

"I need some flies." I replied.

"Tell me what you are looking for?" he asked.

I told him about my idea of creating a special fly for this trip. He called his son-in-law Jay Peck into the conversation. Jay and Carl had worked together harmoniously for a long time. I knew Jay would be the guy doing the tying. You couldn't ask for a better guy. I explained what I wanted. I told them a prominent line in the chorus of the song was, "They got a name for the winners in the world, I want a name when I lose. They call Alabama the crimson tide; call me Deacon blues." And that adding some crimson would be fitting. That perhaps a crimson tail and maybe some in the body would work. They looked at each other and nodded approvingly.

Carl then questioned, "How many do you want?"

"I was thinking about a dozen size 18, a dozen in 16, 14, 12, and 8."

"What about some in size 10?" he asked.

"Well I didn't want to make it too much."

Carl's eyes narrowed. He sensed the catch. "When are you looking to pick these up?"

I said, "As late as Monday morning."

"Three days?" He shook his head while looking at Jay, who had already sketched out a couple of drawings.

"Something like this?" Jay asked.

I told Jay it looked great; I was impressed.

Jay took a moment and said, "I think I can do it. I think I can with the size tens as well. Once you get started, it really doesn't matter about the rest."

I was happy. I smiled at Carl, who was shaking his head. He was smiling, too. Carl knew me. He had taken plenty of short-notice fly orders. I did this sort of thing more than I realized. I actually enjoyed that thought. I could not wait to see how the flies turned out.

The whole trip was a fairly short-notice affair. The kind often described as flying by the seat of your pants. Lots of spontaneity with just enough time to plan some of the major plot points. In the short time for planning, I booked airline tickets, a rental car, and a hotel room for when I would not be at the lodge. Flying is so different for me these days. More than just getting undressed at security checkpoints, I have little to no faith letting the airline people handle important baggage. Not so long ago a rod I was fond of disappeared never to be seen again. Since then, I have started carrying my rods and reels with me. Reels are compact and easy. Rods are big and unwieldy. I have found that I can carry three on a plane but two works out better, incurring far fewer assaults on the other passengers.

If I took the car to Colorado, I could easily take as many as a dozen rods with me. I would drive along with a certain smugness knowing that I had every possible situation covered. A rogue pack of barracudas could present themselves and I would be ready. With only two rods on the trip, see how the imagined smugness turned to a paranoid insecurity? What if that rogue pack showed up?

Choosing the first rod was easy. I received a package a few days earlier from Jerry Kustich of Sweetgrass Rods. It was a stout quadrate bamboo in a four-weight. She was a tad under eight feet and felt so good in my hand. Bamboo rods are a bit like Excalibur, the sword. The rod wants that specific master. It is part of what makes bamboo so special. I was overanxious to fish with it so it was an easy first pick. This made the second pick far more difficult. I had to choose one rod to cover all the other situations that might arise. I have too many rods. I face this truth when someone asks me how many I have or when I have to pick one to cover possible situations that may arise during a trip like this.

As part of the ritual, I go to where I keep my rods. I know them all but it is compulsively necessary to hold them all. Hoping for some portent to help me make a decision. This time, I would not have any such help. Instead, a deliberation over a Scotch and a cigar helped to narrow down the choice. When the smoke cleared, I had chosen a three-piece Winston 6-weight rod. It was a Tom Morgan–era IM6. She is a simple but pretty graphite rod. One of the nice things about her is she makes my casting look good. I call rods like that forgiving. Being a lax Catholic, I try for all the forgiveness I can find. It is interesting that the two rods I chose were products of rebellious Winston rod-makers. Both makers left the corporate culture to pursue a more artistic and free environment in which to ply their craft. I can say that I didn't consciously pick the rods for that reason. I picked rods made by men who did what they could to ditch the rat race to help me ditch the rat race. There are shrinks nodding their heads using the stock line that there are no accidents. It may be what did draw me to those rods in the first place. I could go through my rods and see if a pattern emerges, but I really don't give enough of a shit. Just a quirky observation that was fun to observe.

Packing for the trip was not difficult. I have recently refined this in a way that is competent and simple. I have a bag that I keep packed. It has waders, boots, lanyard, fly bag, and a few other comforts. The fly bag is able to hold eight to ten fly books that I chose based on what I think I need. Occasionally I omit something I really wish I had. The most recent addition is an aluminum Comet coffee pot. It holds two cups and brews a potent and tasty brew. I can fit enough coffee into the body of the maker for a standard five-day trip. I don't drink as much coffee as I used to. My doctor wishes I would drink less Scotch and smoke fewer cigars. I suspect I am heading in that direction but for now the smallish coffee pot is a start. The good news is that is it light and takes up less room than the old eight-cup job.

Time moves so fast. Okay, it moves the exact same speed it has all my life, but it feels fast. I think about how this happens as I am on my way to Coleman's to pick up the custom flies. I wonder how they are going to look. They could be a horror. I have faith in these guys but coming up with a new fly is no easy task. Over time, so many combinations have been tried that something new and effective is tough to achieve. I open the door of the fly shop. Carl is next to the register. I can see a bag with my name on it sitting next to the register on the counter.

"Hi Carl!" I greet my old friend.

"Hello there," he snaps back as is custom with our morning pleasantries.

"I see you have my flies," I say in a relieved tone. This was a tight turnaround. The bag on the counter meant that Jay was equal to the task.

"Yes, sir. Jay did a great job. Come see them."

He pulled the little container cup holding the size eight flies and handed them to me. The first glance took my breath away. I don't usually get so excited about flies, real or synthetic. This was a little different. These were different from anything I could recall but they looked damned fishy. It was a blue-winged olive under-neath. The wings were a tad darker than I usually see. The red tail trailed off behind the body. Almost as if a husk was coming away. The body was dubbed in fine crimson red ribs. They were deli-cately woven into the body so that the whole affair had a crimson overtone. I was sure that the new Deacon Blue-winged Olive was going to catch fish. Even with all these great sentiments percolat-ing in my brain, the only words I could muster were, "Oh, my." Sometimes we fall short in words but the emotion is understood. Carl responded, "Yeah, I know." I paid for the flies and left. I was going from the fly shop to the airport.

The trip required me to fly to Chicago and then on to Denver. Once in Denver I would rent a car and drive to Creede, Colorado. I can remember the days when you could just stroll to the gate, friends and family in tow, and walk onto the plane. In my early days of flying, I can remember smoking at the bar upstairs on the aircraft. It was cool. The largest concern was that it took far less alcohol to get buzzed at thirty-thousand feet. Now we spend large chunks of time standing in line at the security check-in. Surrendering our human dignity for the illusion of safety. The other passengers hide behind their technology while pretending you aren't touching asses and elbows. Flying used to be what you did between work and it could be pleasant. There are still people who fly to escape. You still see parents with children clad in Mickey Mouse ears. Honeymoon couples aglow in the aftermath of sexually charged honeymoons while wearing Don Ho attire. Sometimes tragically unhappy people traveling on the heels of a personal disaster. I recently sat next to a woman who squeezed past me to get to the window seat. Her mascara running down her face and her eyes were wet and swollen. She sat with her face into the window sobbing. If you have lived long enough you can relate. The phone rings at four in the morning. It vibrates through the REM sleep. Your subconscious puts it all together.

You instantly sit up. The ring echoes around your head while you try to contemplate what it could mean. Hours later you find yourself on a plane sobbing in the corner asking God to make it a dream. I looked at her with sympathy. Mercifully, they turned off the lights on the plane. Every now and then, the silence was broken by a low-pitched sob. After a while I told her I was there for here. If she wanted to talk or just hold my hand it would be all right. She looked at me and forced a smile and turned her head back to the window. Later in the flight we encountered some heavy turbulence. I felt a hand grasp mine. I would pat it occasionally with my other hand trying to comfort. The plane landed and she stayed in her seat facing the window until the plane was empty. Sometimes sentience isn't what it is cracked up to be.

Luckily this flight was one where everyone around me ignored one other. I deplaned in Chicago and had to find the departure gate to Denver. Everywhere I looked people were trying to plug in. Every electric outlet in the airport had someone in front of it with all their electronics. Some sitting on designated benches and some sitting on the floor behind a column just to get to the juice to keep plugged in. I couldn't get to the gate fast enough. It seems the closer I get to my escape, the more impatient I become. I found my gate and found myself landing on time in Denver. I was almost free. I left the plane in Denver and boogied down to the luggage carousel. Even a blind squirrel finds an acorn now and then. My acorn was that my bag was coming out just as I got there. I went to the rental-car counter. It had a massive line. It was at least two hours long. I looked at the next rental counter. It was empty. I wondered how much more their rates were. I walked over to find they were twelve dollars a day more. For an extra eighty-four dollars I could avoid a two-hour line. I whipped out my credit card and in a short while I was behind the wheel. I was over the fucking wall. I felt free.

In a short while I was driving south on Route 285. It had been years since I visited southwest Colorado. I remember it being stunningly beautiful, having a pristine quality. I hoped it hadn't been marred by yuppie ambition like Aspen and Steamboat. As I was a couple of hours into the drive, I felt real relief. Remarkably the area had changed very little if at all. The scenery looked like every Western I had ever watched and loved. There is a stretch on 285 that looks like a massive plain ringed by pretty distant mountains. It was so easy to imagine buffalo stretching for miles in any direction. Though you couldn't perceive the altitude, and it was a gradual climb, my lungs could feel it. Denver is called the Mile High city. A quick refresher in measurement conversion has a mile being 5,280 feet above sea level. Broadacres Ranch was a bit over 9,200 feet above sea level. Almost a mile higher than Denver. I live at about 300 feet above sea level, so by the time I pulled into the ranch, the air felt pretty thin.

The ranch sits just a couple of miles outside of Creede, a town where neither a stop light nor fast-food franchise is anywhere in sight. I liked that so much. Situated in the heart of the San Juan Mountains, it stays pure, untainted by corporate America. I could feel the coils of oppression slip off as I pulled into the lodge office. Pulling in right behind me was Bruce Tweeten, along with his pretty wife, Jody. Bruce is a touch over six feet and a fit one hundred and ninety pounds. He had on his cowboy duds. It wasn't a costume, but rather work clothes. Jody was a tiny woman with a warm smile. Together they were a team. Something becoming more common these days—married couples hired as a team to run a ranch. It is a smart strategy and seems to work.

As I checked in, Bruce said that I had brought the rain with me. He told me how rare rain is in this semi-arid country. A place where the growing season seldom exceeded sixty days. Alongside the Rio Grande were five private cabins with covered porches and rocking swings that overlooked the river. They were each named after a trout fly. My cabin was the Blue Quill. It was a two-bedroom cabin with a bathroom. It also sported a fine little kitchen area complete with 1950s-style furnishings of chrome and vinyl. On the counter was a very nice welcome basket. It had the compulsory stuff: coffee mug, key chain, flashlight, pen, and a few other knickknacks, including a beautiful oak fly box with the ranch name and logo etched into it. Upon further inspection of the cabin, there was no television, which is good, and no internet, which was okay, too. The cell phone worked and that was good. I would easily unplug while being unreachable. There was a knock at the door. It was Bruce with some fresh baked cookies and milk. He handed me the goodies and told me to come to the lodge the next morning. I wolfed the cookies and chugged the milk. I slept like the dead.

The following morning had me taking a short walk to the main lodge. Over the door was a carved sign that read "Glenmora." She was a stunning lodge. As you walked through the door, there was a stocked bar. Across the way was a warm and well-crafted fireplace. Past that was a dining room with all the tables set in fine linen and silverware. It stood on the ready for the guests who would arrive the following week. One small table against the window overlooking the Rio Grande had two glasses of ice water, indicating where I would sit. I sat looking at the river as she roared with water the color of chocolate milk pushing over her banks. At that moment, Bruce came in and sat across from me.

"I don't think we will be fishing her today," I said as I pointed to the angry waters.

"No," Bruce said. "See that peak up there?" He pointed to a tall mountain. "That's where the runoff for the Rio comes from. Lots more snow up there than yesterday. It rained here but snowed there."

I was wondering if I had made a mistake. It was as if Bruce could read my thoughts. He told me, "I was out looking at water this morning. The small creek that runs into the lakes is running a bit high, but it is clear and fishable."

Jody came to the table and asked us for our breakfast preference. I asked for some pancakes and bacon. I love pancakes on fishing trips. I seldom eat them otherwise but I found myself there wanting a fat stack and hoping for real maple syrup. As Jody left to prepare breakfast, Bruce informed me that the regular chef had something come up and would not be able to work at the lodge this summer. Jody was going to try to get the gig and I was going to be her guinea pig for the trip. That probably sounds a little ominous, but it wasn't. It turned out that she was a marvelous chef and it was the best lodge food I had ever had. Every meal was a culinary delight. I am not sure if she got the job but if she didn't, that would be a colossal mistake. The pancakes were light and fluffy and the syrup was one hundred percent authentic maple syrup.

After breakfast, I rigged up the quadrate bamboo rod. I tied on a Deacon Blue-winged Olive. I wanted to get that monkey off my back, straight away. It turned out the small creek was running quite fast. You barely had time to mend your line before the fly was out of the small pools. The takes were quick and reflexes needed to be equal to get a hook set. I did get into a certain rhythm and was rewarded with a dozen or so nice brown trout in the 12–14-inch range. As we fished downstream toward the lake, the pools deepened and widened. The fishing slowed to more normal proportions. The effort was rewarded with another dozen browns of similar stature. I was happy that not only had I broken the ice with the special fly, it was doing well.

There were four lakes on the property. Two were small, what I would call ponds. I never really understood the difference between ponds and lakes, streams, creeks, and rivers; it seems to depend on where you are at as much as size and physical criteria. Then there were the larger waters, ones that I would apply my

Northeastern standards to and call lakes. No one ever mentioned names and would call them the big lake and the smaller lake. If anything it pointed to how little they were fished. As we stood at the inlet to the smaller lake, Bruce confirmed my suspicion. "We don't fish these much," he said. "I do know they have lots of small browns. You can see them when you drive along the shore."

We fished the shore for the rest of the morning. It was a frustrating affair. There was so much growth along the banks that I decorated more than a few trees with pretty little flies. The good news was that where and when you could place a well-presented fly, it was rewarded with a scrappy brown trout. At about the time my frustration was at its peak, a quick-moving thunderstorm wailed into us. It was a cold driving rain with heavy cracks of thunder and lighting. We took cover next to one of the finely-decorated trees until it was obvious that we needed to get into the truck. It was a little past lunchtime so we headed back for lunch. It was hard to complain as we had landed at least three dozen pretty brown trout. I would consider that a good day anywhere.

In the truck, I said to Bruce, "Boy, it would be so much easier to fish that lake with a boat."

Bruce looked at me. He placed his hand on his chin. His mouth opened and shut several times. He has something on his mind, I thought. Something he wasn't sure about. "What?" I said, hoping to shake loose whatever it was he was struggling with.

"I have a boat," he said with some hesitancy. "I am not sure if you will like it. It's not much of a boat." His cowboy drawl had me hanging on each syllable as it slowly came forth. "I mean it's small and old. Doesn't look very good."

"Does it float?" I said in my New York way. "Look, man, if we can fish from it count me in." I looked at him with a big smile waiting for him to commit.

"Okay," he said. "We can try it."

We pulled up to the lodge and had a hearty lunch. The rain kept coming. Bruce told me to go and relax at my cabin and he would get the boat together. I went to my cabin and sat in the swing under the covered porch. I lit a cigar and stared at the chocolate-colored water. I would occasionally glance at the mountain peak Bruce pointed out earlier. It seemed that the snow cover was growing. I wasn't sure where this trip was going. The morning did produce some fine fishing. We worked for them, but we caught them. I put some ice in a glass and put some single malt over the ice. By the time Bruce showed up two hours later, I was ready to fish.

I hopped in the pickup. I noticed Bruce's Stetson was soaked. He had been out in the rain the whole time doing something. When we reached the lake, I could see what he had been doing. On the bank was a boat. Sort of. It was an old Johnboat, fifties vintage. It was a 6½-foot aluminum job with most of the green-ish blue paint chipped away. Attached across the back with several screw clamps was a board and attached to the board was a trolling motor. I understood Bruce's earlier apprehension. It was some-thing. I wondered if it was going to float with two big guys in it. As I mentioned earlier, Bruce was over six foot and maybe a fit one hundred and ninety pounds, I was over six foot and a chunky two hundred and fifty pounds. We climbed into the boat and it did float. We sighed a sigh of relief in perfect harmony. Hell, we were a full 6 inches above the water. I sat there with my fly bag between my feet. Bruce gingerly pushing us along with the troll-ing motor. It wasn't pretty, but it was working. The rain finally quit and we were fishing in earnest. In the absence of rises Bruce suggested something like a Wooly Bugger in black. I went into my bag and found a size eight with black rabbit fur, a brass bead head, and some red Flashabou.

"I was afraid to show you the boat," Bruce said.

"I can see why," I said and laughed.

"It's not that bad." He smiled. "I paid seventy-five bucks for her. She was never meant for guests. I got her to help with chores around here. We never fish these lakes."

As he said that, a fish hit the fly, a nice brown. A few minutes later, another nice brown. It began to heat up, almost a fish every cast. I lay down a pretty cast and the fly was immediately crushed. For the briefest of moments, I felt something a little bigger than the fish we had been catching. The line went slack, and my fish and fly were gone. I tied on the same pattern and we kept catching more fish. Most were 16–18 inches with the occasional 20 thrown in. Then it happened again. Hard hit followed by broken leader. I was starting to wonder what the hell it was. I tied on what turned out to be the last of that fly pattern I had. We boated fish after fish. I am sure we were a sight to behold, but who cared? I was having a legendary afternoon. I was sure we had boated at least a hundred fish. Shortly after thinking that, I had another hard hit. This time the knot and leader held. Then the fish did a little tail walking. It was a big beautiful rainbow trout. It is precisely these moments that flyfishermen live for, when we hook into a big, mean son of a bitch, a fish that tests the core of the sport. Will the 4-weight quadrate bamboo rod from Jerry at Sweetgrass Rods hold and handle the fish? Will the Peerless reel's smooth drag do its job? Will I be able to take these quality works made by the caring hands of master craftsmen and use them skillfully? Will my guide use his skills to maneuver this bathtub of a boat to keep the correct angle to the fish? In this moment it all comes together. It is the convergence of all the points of this sport to one moment in time that's the test of our mettle, the moment of truth that comes rarely and in its own time. It is these times, especially, with bamboo that light my fire.

In the course of minutes, the fish eased into the net. This time everything worked like it was supposed to. The big rainbow trout was subdued. She was in the net, beautiful and tired.

This was a fish to be measured in pounds instead of inches. The scale tells the tale, and she was a hair over 4½ pounds. A giant by Rocky Mountain standards. After a few photos I gently and reverently returned her to her water. It is proper to sit and bask in the moment. I pondered how well the rod performed. It is truly a piece of art. I recall feeling each thrust of the fish's tail coming down through the rod, through the cork grip and into the touch of my fingers that sent impulse to my brain causing endorphins to flow. The reel's smooth drag took over almost instantly after hookset. My guide struggled mightily against the beast of the boat. Me, being the angler, like a good conductor over a talented symphony, orchestrated it all into the height of fly-fishing sport. What a high.

Bruce broke my contemplative trance with the announcement that the killer fly was mangled. It was the last of its kind. I tied on a bevy of different flies with varying shades of mediocrity. It seems cliché that the hot fly runs out. If you think about it, then it makes sense. It is working well, drawing aggressive strikes that shortens the life of the lure. I usually try to put a few of everything in my fly bag. It covers a range of options but offers little depth in any one pattern. It is times like this that good tiers really have an advantage. Having lived a lifetime as a poor tier, you learn to sniff them out. On my way to the lodge, I did make a mental note of a couple nice-looking fly shops.

"How are those fly shops in town?" I asked Bruce.

"They are really great. I think you'll be impressed. Lots and lots of flies." He tended toward being slow and conservative in his conversation. So his quantifying the amount of flies as "Lots and lots" had me jazzed up.

"Let's hit them up right after breakfast," I said as I figured it was worth trying to find a replacement of the hot fly.

The following morning, we headed to town after more pancakes. Driving around a town and actually walking around town are very different. Walking allows you to pick up nuances not possible in a drive-by. Creede, Colorado is a special place. It has quaint shops and local stores. The highest compliment you can give a place is to say that you could live there. I could live in Creede. Both shops were what fly shops are supposed to be: A place that supports the greatest sport on the planet and not a place that supports your position in status-symbol land. One of the shops had lots and lots of flies. Hundreds if not thousands of patterns. I quickly found something very similar to the "hot" fly. It had the brass bead head and the black bunny fur. It had the red Flashabou, too. The only appreciable difference was that it had a touch of green Flashabou, as well. We all know that small changes in a fly can mean the difference between feast or famine. It took me quite some time to be able to leave the shop. If Superman has kryptonite and Batman has Robin, my weakness is a fly shop that actually has flies. I am what you call old school.

By the time we actually made it back to the ranch, it was lunchtime. After lunch we rode down to the smaller pond and squeezed into the S.S. *Tub*. I had replaced the light leader with a stouter one. I tied on the new fly and in a short time picked up where we left off. The fly worked every bit as good as its predecessor, maybe a little better. Again after fishing a while, dark clouds started to head our way. As they got closer, the fishing just kept getting better. I had already burned up a couple of flies, but it didn't matter. In a rare situation, I had the right fly in ample supply. As it happened the previous day, as the nasty weather set in, the fishing caught fire. Bruce kept reminding me that this was semi-arid country and rain was rare. I would chuckle because I had seen plenty of precipitation since I arrived. Bruce chuckled as well, telling me that I must have had the rain follow me from the East. We had caught so many trout. As the weather worsened I had a fish on that felt a bit different. We had caught plenty of browns and rainbows but this had a different but familiar feel.

My suspicions were confirmed as a pretty 18-inch brook trout came to the net. The fish looked alien to me. It had a large head proportionate to its body. It had a deep kype in its jaw. It took a moment but I figured it out. The big head with a pipe like body behind it. It was nothing like the other brook trout I was used to catching, with a deep belly and healthy look. This was a really old brook trout. You never see an old brook trout. They just taste too damned good. I guessed this fish was a dozen years old. It probably was a holdover from the last time the lake was stocked. I did catch several more on the trip and each one just struck me. It was a real experience to see ancient brook trout.

It was shortly after the time we released that old trout that the weather asserted itself. High winds and whitecaps can create peril. Usually I try to hang in there but thunder and lightning is something I don't mess with. We came off the water. We had caught more trout than I could keep track of. We headed back to the lodge. We decided that I would rest while Bruce attended to some chores. Then we would go back out after dinner.

Dinner was a four-star culinary event. We went out afterwards, too. The hot spots on the smaller lake were still good, but the fishing was not as productive as earlier. It turns out the water "police" had shut some of the gates that fed water to the lake. Being from the Great Lakes region, it's hard for me to grasp that water is a precious and scarce commodity in many places, and it's carefully measured in cubic feet and controlled to be fair to all the landowners. This closure definitely reduced the flow into the lake. The inlets that produced a fish almost on every cast waned down to a trickle and to a fish every fourth or fifth cast. You would have to be a real asshole to complain, though.

Something unusual happened that evening. After a pretty cast that induced a heavy take—I mean a jolt that makes you say "Okay, fuck" to yourself—I was into a big fish. The kind of fish that I just couldn't move with the 4-weight bamboo rod. I usually fish my bamboo rods with extreme confidence. I have only ever broken two. One fell victim to a car door. I think the car door thing is a rite of passage. Almost all my "boo" friends have done it at least once; this risk makes flyfishermen become more careful. The other breakage was on a fish, but it was a case of bad bamboo. The rod broke just above the grip and you could see rotted bamboo.

Now I was fighting a big fish, and to throw all caution to the wind would be foolish. A bamboo fly rod is still blades of grass—expensive blades of grass, so you make sure to match the rod to the situation. I am told that you can always break off a fish that's too big. That is like saying, "I enjoy sex, but I try to stop before I have an orgasm." My epitaph would read, "He came and he went." It is just not in my nature to break off a fish, although since I boast of only two broken rods it is only fair that I mention the half dozen or so with bent tips. So much memory is set into the bamboo tip that it is beyond repair. The bent tips bolster memories.

Knowing the limits of the bamboo rod, I still pushed the envelope on that big fish. All you can really do is try to play the fish and hope it tires before something gives out. In the case of this fish, the hook straightened and the fish was gone. I lost the battle. I reeled in the line defeated. I promptly broke down the bamboo rod. She was undamaged. I wish I could say the same for my ego. I would switch to a graphite rod to fish the lakes from then on. Who knew what size that fish was? It would haunt me for the whole night. All I could do was hope that the fly-fishing gods would give me another chance. I started looking at the lakes with all the wonderment that any real enigma demands.

At breakfast the following morning, Bruce asked me if I would like to fish up high. I told him I'd really like that. I always like the pristine nature that comes with fishing at altitude. I gathered my things after breakfast and we were going to Rat Creek for some alpine brook-trout fishing. I love brook trout. Fishing for them at the top of the world has real appeal. I met Bruce at the truck and we were on our way. We went past town and were soon at the silver mines. It was a hell of a sight. The mines were dormant but in shape, miners waiting for silver prices to rise high enough to resume mining. The fire department was housed entirely in an old shaft and the local government in another. There were modern structures as well as very old ones. The old structures were mind-blowing, looking as if they were tacked onto the side of the steep mountain. It was surreal looking. Not far from the main shaft were cabins from the 1800s. They were small, which made me realize how cold and brutal the winters must be. Shortly after that the paved roads gave way to gravel, then dirt. They spiraled upward for almost an hour. In time, we came to a small blue ribbon of a water called Rat Creek. The lodge stood at just over 9,200 feet above sea level, and this was at least three thousand feet above that.

I've done a fair amount of elk hunting in the west. Altitude never really bothered me. I have learned to breathe slow and deep, and I can recall only one instance of altitude sickness. The air was thin but it seemed to make up for that with a certain kind of purity that tasted sweet. I decided to fish the bamboo rod. It just seemed right. I tied on the Deacon Blue-Winged Olive pattern in a size 12. The stream was loaded with pods of beautiful brook trout. These fish were small, most four to six inches. An eight-inch fish was rare. What they lacked in size, they over compensated for with beauty. Every hue was exaggerated as if they were electric. The vermiculation was crisp and well-defined. More than once, I caught myself just staring at the diminutive fish. A wiggle would snap me out of my funk and I would realize the little guys really wanted back into the water. You could catch them at will as long as you avoided casting a shadow over the water.

I was at the top of the world, occasionally trouncing through snow that seemed to have a real shot at surviving the summer. At one point, a discerning marmot whistled at me. If you've never seen a marmot, think of a ground hog crossed with a badger. They live near or above the tree line and whistle to sound the alarm when an intruder stomps through. After a while, when he figured I was not a threat, he stopped whistling, curious about the strange creature waving a stick over the water making small trout fly. I'm sure I caught him smiling at the sight. I caught trout at will. After a while I could feel the smile muscles on my face starting to tire. If there is a prelude to heaven this might be it.

A few hours into the fishing, the dark clouds that followed me all week started heading at me again. We decided to go back to the truck and eat lunch on the tailgate. The climb uphill to the truck took a while. I had to stop every fifty feet to do what I could to recover my wind. Eventually I made it to the truck. We ate lunch. I was anxious to get to a lower elevation. The place took my breath away in a couple of ways. I remember chatting with Bruce and then I remember waking up as we pulled into the ranch. I felt good. It is amazing how you can start to feel good when the yoke is lifted. We discussed what we would do next: We would fish the big lake.

We took a break, and later that afternoon Bruce picked me up. I didn't know what to expect, but I was jazzed up. So far everything had been so fishy. What could the big lake hold? I know—thinking like that can lead to disappointment.

We got to the big lake, and I had the graphite rod strung up, ready for anything. Bruce had moved the S.S. *Tub* to that shore. The fishing turned out to be even better than the smaller lake— the fish were bigger and fought harder. Bruce apologized for not being able to fish the Rio. I looked at him in amazement. To complain or to be disappointed would be obscene. That morning I easily caught more brook trout than I ever remember doing. They were small, but special. Now I was on the big lake catching plenty of almost 20-inch brown and rainbow trout.

In what was becoming a daily ritual, the dark clouds we spotted at Rat Creek were coming straight for us. It was becoming a running joke, we were like five-year-olds on a long car ride who just discovered the magic of knock-knock jokes. High winds and cold rain sometime were accompanied with thunder and lightning, but the fish were turned on into a feeding frenzy.

The sky continued to darken and the wind was coming harder and faster. Gusts had to be well over 40 miles an hour. The fishing was getting as wild as the weather. As the pace picked up, the size of fish increased, as well: 2–3 pound rainbows were hitting the fly with regularity. The smile muscles on my face were hurting again. The wind kept coming. Bruce was struggling with boat control. My fly was a mangled mess. I tied on a fresh fly. Bruce was screaming something at me into the wind.

"What?" I screamed back.

"I can't get the boat into the shore!" he screamed. The poor little trolling motor was losing ground.

"Okay," I screamed over the wind. "I'll try to paddle."

Then some lighting flickered. Time to get my rig in the boat. I laid out a cast with the wind. It went to my right and behind me a bit. It was my plan to cast all the line out and reel it in neatly and then help with boat control. There are times when the fishing gods need to prove they have a sense of humor. That cast, which I made only to help get the line in, was met by a fierce strike. The wind was howling, the rain was driving hard and the lights were flickering. All hell was breaking loose. I screamed at Bruce, "I have a fish on and I think it might be a good one!"

Then it happened: A sound most fishermen rarely hear. It was like a beaver swatting its tail on the water, or the sound of a fat man doing a belly flop, or the sound of a big fish breaking the water's surface and coming down with a thunderous, *slap*! The fish was behind us. Our priorities changed at once. The sound, the thundering *slap*, shot through me. It permeated my spine and at once passed through the cortex of my brain. I looked up at Bruce and as my eyes met his I knew he was thinking the exact same thing. It is a sound that echos through the subconscious of all serious fishermen's brains.

In a moment, Bruce maneuvered the *Tub* to a better angle. As if on cue, the fish showed herself with another jump and a slap equal to the first. Whitecaps lapping over the side of the boat, terrific gusts of wind, perilous thunder and lightning all went unnoticed. We were riveted on the battle taking place before our eyes. The fish kept taking to the air in a violent attempt to get free. I thought how glad I was that I left the bamboo home. Then my brain began to worry about the 6-weight graphite. No words were spoken. We had enough experience and worked together as good as any guide and client could. Every jump and every roll gave us a better view of the giant fish. *My God,* I thought as endorphins and adrenalin rushed through me.

There is a time in every epic battle when the outcome is completely uncertain. Guide and client were thinking the same thing: "Let us land this fish!" The silence hung in the air. I could feel Brian's struggle with the unwieldy boat. In the kind of eternity that fills up moments, the fish came alongside the boat. Brian held the net in his hands waiting for the opportunity. Looking at the net and the fish, we both were estimating whether the fish would fit. In a moment, Bruce scooped at the fish, with the phrase "Oh, fuck" crossing his lips. I held my breath. In one big scooping motion the fish entered the net with its tail hanging out. Then it flipped out of the net into the bottom of the boat. We began whooping and hollering. Splashing through six inches of water to high five each other. Then in the next instant we were drawn back to the situation at hand. We were in the middle of a lake about to be battered by a bombastically violent thunderstorm.

The fish was obviously a beautiful rainbow trout with pretty stripes of rose and green. An iridescent sheen with black flecking covered a deep body. Bruce struggled to get the fish weighed. She was just shy of 7 pounds. We started cheering again. Bruce was in shock. He'd had no idea that fish like this were in the lake, hiding in plain sight.

The weather quickly forced us to get serious. Bruce released the prize carefully and unharmed. It was time to go. During the fight, the wind had blown us across the lake. The truck was a speck on the far shore. Trying to move along with the trolling motor was futile. The only choice we had was to stay close to shore and hoof it around to the other side of the lake. Things became even more serious as lightning struck close. Luckily, we made shore quickly after deciding to go with the wind. In the storm, we bailed the boat, and now it was barely above water. We were able to pull her out of the lake and turn her over. It took almost an hour to get to the truck.

The hike to the truck could have been miserable, but we were bolstered by the great fight. We talked about it all on the way to the truck. We knew that a day like this is one that gets burned deep into memory cells. To be recalled time and again. Becoming part of our personal fishing legends. By the time we reached the truck, the wet and cold had gone deep into my bones and I continued to shiver all the way back to the ranch. Bruce dropped me off in front of my cabin. We both were smiling broad smiles. We exchanged a few more moments of maleness and testosterone and said good night.

I went right into a hot shower. The hot water loosened tight muscles and took the chill out of my bones. I sat there under the showerhead basking in triumph. You don't get many days like this, so I feel it's okay to gloat and soak it in. As I was drying myself, I noticed I was still shaking. I decided to pour a small glass of Scotch and my hands trembled during the pour. What I assumed were shivers from the cold driving rain was really the effect of all the adrenalin. I hope that catching a big fish will always have that effect on me. Beautiful, primal emotions fuel my inner outdoorsman; God, I love this sport. Sleep came easy.

The following morning, I still felt the residuals from the previous day's excitement. I sauntered over to breakfast—saunter is what flyfisherman do instead of walking for about two days after a major historical/hysterical event—and as I got to the breakfast table Bruce was there, aglow with that broad cowboy smile that I was really getting used to. Fly fishing is as close as some people get to an actual sport. In my case, my time in the outdoors is as close as I have been to a sport since my early thirties. What happened the day before—withstanding an epic storm to subdue a sea-monster trout—counts as a great feat in the annals of my fly fishing. Bruce and I were in full strut.

This is the kind of thing that the fishing gods usually want to correct, I have to acknowledge.

That morning a big, fluffy stack of pancakes smothered in maple syrup tasted great. The air was extra sweet. We discussed where we were going to fish. I was amazed that the conversation was even happening. I sometimes forget that there is a segment of the fly-fishing brotherhood that looks down their noses at fishing still water. I think Bruce was being sensitive to that ideology. The Rio Grande was running higher and dirtier than the day I arrived. All the rain I seem to have brought with me made sure of that. Even if she was running slow and clear, I couldn't walk away from the big lake. I couldn't even think of doing anything else. I wanted to, at that time, more than anything else, fish that big lake all day. Bruce admitted that he was hoping I would say that. He had been there for a few years. With the upper Rio Grande being so good, nobody ever even looked at the lake. We were both intrigued. What else could be there?

The fishing after breakfast was as good as it gets. We were burning through flies. Some spots were hot spots: You would fish them until they cooled a bit and then go on to the next spot. Rinse and repeat. We caught dozens of trout, mostly rainbows, with the occasional brown trout and then rarely a brook trout. Before lunch we had caught and landed at least four dozen between 16–24 inches. Holy shit. In most cases it would be hard to leave fishing like that. We had caught so many fish that it was easy to be cavalier about it, and Jody's cooking was just getting better and better. It would have been tough to miss one of her meals. Luckily we didn't have to—we did both, fished and ate well. When life gets this good, I wait for the other shoe to drop.

After lunch, we piled into the S.S. *Tub* and the fishing resumed where it had left off. By midafternoon the wind started to pick up and off in the distance, sure enough, heading right toward us were the black clouds. It was becoming our routine. As the storm drew nearer the fishing heated up. As during the days before, when the weather erupted so did the fishing. I had just replaced a tired, chewed up fly with a shiny new one. That's when it happened. I had a monstrous take, at the moment Bruce was fighting the elements again. I drew back to set the hook. I wanted to make sure I set it solid. I drew back and the fly came whizzing back toward the boat. *Smack*, the impact echoed above the gushing wind and driving rain. "OH FUCK!" echoed above the gushing wind and driving rain. I turned toward the guide to see the fly buried into the knuckle above the thumb on Bruce's left hand. It was something I had worried about when we first got into the boat practically in each other's lap. I tried to cast so carefully. Ironically it happened while I was trying to hook a fish.

I was horrified. In my whole life, I had avoided snagging the guide. Now here we were, and to make matters worse I forgot to pinch down the barb. The hook was firmly implanted well above the barb. I did what I could to help. I had read the literature on how to remove a hook by holding the eye flat against the skin and to pull it out with a loop of monofilament. Bruce squirmed like a boy in a dentist chair. I was dying of embarrassment while at the same time torturing the guide. In his infinite patience, he pushed me aside, took a pair of needle nose pliers and ripped the fly out of his hand. By this time there was blood everywhere. He thrust his hand into the cool water while I was figuring how much extra I would have to add to the tip for combat pay. By this time the weather was a full-blown gale. I asked him if he wanted to go back.

"The battery is dead on the trolling motor," he screamed above the din.

"I am so sorry!" I screamed back. I felt bad.

"I'll be okay," he shouted to me. "Let's let the wind take us to the far shore and we'll hoof it like we did yesterday." I remained silent. Truly ashamed by what happened. It is the kind of thing guides share with each other when they start telling bad-client stories.

While we were waiting for the storm to blow us to shore, I would alternate between casting and bailing the boat. That next cast had me pulling back on a solid hit. I noticed Bruce lower his profile. "Aw, shit," I said under my breath. The fish ended up being hooked. The whole affair started off slowly. As the fight progressed, the fish seemed to grow. In moments the rod was doubled over and I was into my backing. Bruce changed his attention from his thumb to the situation at hand. The fish would not jump. It just dug and pulled. Being the tough cowboy that he is, Bruce picked up the paddle and started working the boat. Slowly I would gain line and quickly the fish would take it back. It was quite a fight. We had reached the far shore and the fish was still not showing itself. Bruce asked, "Is it a snapping turtle?"

I shouted I didn't know. "I think I saw a flash of silver," I said.

By this time, we were both in the water. Bruce standing with his net as I struggled to keep the rod tip high. As more time passed, an exhausted fish came to the surface on its side. Bruce slid the net under the giant fish. In the net was the most beautiful brown trout I had ever seen. The sides were adorned with a streak the color of butternut squash. It had red dots and black spots all haloed with a bluish grey. Most distinguished of all was the two shimmering green stripes running the length of the fish. Those green stripes make Colorado browns the most beautiful of all brown trout. The large size of the fish exaggerates the coloration. On the scale, the big pretty girl, was an honest 5½ pounds. I was in awe. Bruce was snapping photos. For the second day in a row the lake gave us the ultimate gift in fly fishing.

We whooped it up again. We were soaked to the bone again. We were fly-fishing gods again. We got back to my cabin and my hands trembled as I poured two glasses of Scotch. We lit two cigars and basked in the glory of this blessing. You seldom get a trip like this. Even the guide was amazed. After the *ad hoc* party, I cleaned up and nestled into my bed. I opened the window and could feel the cool breeze. It was in the fifties in the room. I like to sleep cold. The cool mountain air, along with visions of big fish, eased me into sleep the same way we eased the caught fish back into the cool water.

The next morning was the beginning of the final day at the Broadacres Ranch. It would be my last stack of pancakes for a while. Bruce and I discussed the previous day. We decided to skip the morning. It would allow me to pack and Bruce to chase down some errands. It also would allow us to fish after dinner— to see if there was an opportunity to cast dry flies to rising fish on the big lake.

After lunch we decided to see how many big trout we could catch. By saying *big* we meant fish over three pounds. We found a couple of places where the big rainbows seemed to hang out.

The fishing was as good as it had been all week. The time was less hectic and had an old slow feel to it. It gave us a chance to talk about the ranch. Bruce mentioned that they tried to keep it to five or six rods per week. The main attraction was fishing the

Rio. We then started talking about the ownership. The owner was a successful entrepreneur type. A bit of a maverick who had a real love for cars. That explained all the crazy vehicles strewn all over the property. At first you would believe they were left there from days gone by. It made far more sense that someone placed them there to be dealt with at a later time. Charles Nearburg loves vehicles and speed. When you enter the lodge there are cards to be taken. They feature Charles and his "Spirit of Rett." It is the fastest single-engine car in history. Its speed of 422.645 miles per hour is a world record. He has about a dozen more speed records. Charles doesn't just put the cars and the team together, he is the driver as well.

Charles founded the ranch with his son Rett. It was something they shared and fell in love with. Together, father and son started molding and building a dream. A courageous young man, Rett battled cancer and in his early twenties, and was taken from the people who loved him. As a cancer survivor myself, the story struck a chord with me. His father carried on with the ranch as a monument to his son. You can feel the love of the father all over the ranch. It explained so much. The driving force of the ranch was not money, it was love. It gives the ranch a special quality that would be near impossible to duplicate. It was catching lightning in a bottle. I never got to meet Charles, but I know I would like him.

That afternoon, Bruce and I talked about many things. I really got to feel a bond with him. Later that afternoon, as if on cue, the dark clouds started rolling in. They weren't as violent as the previous days. A gentle shower came with mild winds. As in days before, the fishing heated up. It never reached the point where we felt we needed to leave the lake. We caught fish and continued to chat. I told Bruce how nice it would be to have a better boat. I imagined fishing the lake with my Grand Lake Stream canoe. Matching things of beauty just seemed to make sense. We met our goal that afternoon. We boated more than thirty rainbow trout over three pounds. In my life, I can only recall two or three trips that could equal this one.

After supper, we went out to sit in the S.S. *Tub* one last time. I tied on the special fly for the trip, a size 8 Deacon Blue-Winged Olive. We chased rises that evening until the light started to fade. As the sun slipped behind the horizon, it threw up beams of gold shining through distant clouds illuminated in hues of pink and purple. While Bruce was taking the motor, oars, and other equipment that we used off the boat, I walked over to the inlet. The small stream that flowed into the lake had three sweet pools just above the inlet. I had seen some rises and like a drunk that sets the bottle on its side to squeeze that last drops of spirits from the vessel, I cast my fly into the reflection of the sunset. At once a large head poked out from under the surface and slurped my fly. Minutes later I slid the fish up on the bank. I held in my hands a gorgeous 22-inch cutthroat trout. The blazing red slashes on her gill plate just seemed to blend in with the stunning mountain sunset. Though there was time for a few more casts, I clipped the fly from my line and started breaking down my rod. It was a great ending for my time on the ranch.

The following morning, I loaded up my rental car and walked over to the lodge. It had been a hell of a trip. So far. There was the trip to Red Rock yet to come. I said my goodbyes to Bruce and Jody. Apologized for being a pain in the ass—and pain in the thumb. Minutes later, I was through the town of Creede and on the road again. I played highlights of the week in my mind. Catching four kinds of trout in a surprise way. Who goes all the way to a cabin on the banks of the upper Rio Grande to fish a couple of unknown lakes? I love when adventures take on a life of their own.

It was a five-hour trip to the hotel where I was staying near Red Rocks. I thought about turning on the television. It had been the better part of a week since I had. There was something in me that didn't want to. I pulled out my Surface Pro and logged onto my email account. I had told everyone I cared about I was off the grid for a week. Even so, I had more than two hundred emails. I looked down the list and it didn't take long to realize it was the same old horse shit. I shut the computer down. It made me recall a time not so long ago without cable television, cell phones, internet, personal computers, GPS, and Twitter. George Orwell's *1984* came right when expected.

I decided to lay out my clothes for the concert the following day. I had a really faded pair of Lee jeans. They were soft in a way that it takes at least five years of proper wearing to get there. I used to wear tie-dyed T-shirts to concerts in the old days. I somehow felt that I might be too old to wear them in public. Instead, I brought white dress shirts, and sent them to a guy who professionally tie-dyes them. That was it—a faded pair of jeans, a tie-dyed dress shirt, and a pair of grey suede shoes, I was ready for the concert.

I am not really sure where I fit in the demographics of America. Born in 1963, I sometimes get thrown in with the boomers and at other times with Generation X. It depends on whose view of history you accept. I remember a conversation I had with a friend while we were in our late teens. "Who do we listen to: Timothy Leary and 'Turn on, Tune in, Drop out' or Nancy Reagan and 'Just say no!'?" I thought about it for a bit, and finally replied "Fuck 'em both!"

It took all of five minutes to prepare for the following day. I had the rest of the night to kill. I ordered a pizza and soda. I went to my bag and pulled out Khalil Gibran's *The Prophet*. I had read it several times before. If some guy can watch *Star Wars* 147 times, I can reread *The Prophet* all I want. I was interrupted by a poor version of a pizza delivered by a national chain. After that, I almost read the book from cover to cover. I woke up in the middle of the night fully dressed with the book on my chest. I liked escaping. It is good for my soul.

I slept in until the afternoon. My body was tired. I picked up the book and finished it off. When I set it on the nightstand, it was time to go to Red Rocks. I had been to Red Rocks many times in my life. It still was an amazing sight as I rounded the corner into the natural amphitheater. It's like walking into the Sistine Chapel, you can just feel a greater presence.

I found my seat, a perfect front-row-center seat. I looked behind me. Past the grass field loaded with thousands of people. People with grey hair and bent backs. My people. The first thing I thought when I saw them was these are the "survivors." Those folks whose bodies held up to a lifestyle that brought a constant thinning of the herd. As I looked past all that, I saw the presence that had been following me from when I first arrived in Colorado: the mass of black thunderheads.

Knowing that it might get rough, I went to the concession stand and purchased one of those "reusable" plastic ponchos. It was reusable only if you could refold it correctly and place it back into the plastic envelope it came in. It made refolding a roadmap seem easy. In my case, they were clearly disposable.

By the time Steve Winwood took the stage, the black mass had rolled in. Steve looked thin in his windbreaker. He sat at the keyboard and the wind started coming. By the time he had started to his third song, Blind Faith's "Can't Find My Way Home," all hell broke loose.

The wind and driving rain was blowing equipment off the stage. Steve deepened his resolve and stood from the keyboards. He was at center stage leaning his frail sixty-eight-year-old frame in defiance into the gale. The gusts were easily topping fifty miles per hour. It was a war of wills, man against nature. As the weather grew worse, Steve's voice grew in intensity: "You are the reason I've been waiting so long, somebody holds the key."

The survivors sensing the poignancy of the moment stood in defiance, cheering and letting Steve know that we were in it together. By the time Steve blasted out the last line, "And I'm wasted and can't find my way home," the weather was in full roar. Hail the size of Shooter Aggies (a type of marble, for those of you who never played) pounded everything. They ushered Steve Winwood off the stage. Then made announcements and posted notice on the electronic sign boards that the concert wasn't cancelled and that everyone should go back to their cars. We would be notified when the concert would resume.

Ten thousand people trying to leave the amphitheater, through two bottlenecked corridors, was a sight. Being in the front row had me at the stage left bottleneck. I was not only stuck but also suddenly could feel the uncontrollable force of a crowd pushing. I suddenly knew how European soccer fans feel before being in peril of being trampled. I screamed "*STOP pushing, this is how people get hurt!*" And as if I was a voice of reason from above, they listened. I felt like I needed to follow it up with some instructions. "*Just hunker down against the people around you. It will blow over!*" It was incredible, they listened again. It was an odd yet enjoyable feeling of control. People are strange.

I started to take my own advice. I made a tent out of the poncho. I used my right hand to hold the hood tight and straight out. Using my right hand on one end, and my shoulders on the other, I was marginally protected. The hail came harder and more fiercely. As each stinging pelt hit my body, I could feel the welts raising and the blood pooling under newly formed bruises. I remember thinking, "Is this what I wanted when I decided to escape?" I recalled all the trout, pretty scenery, and even the current feeling of being really alive. "Hell yes!" I wouldn't trade any of it for anything. It was at about that moment that a security guard clad in black and gold told people to follow him. He led us to a long corridor back stage.

There were hundreds of people crowded into the long corridor behind the stage. In that corridor, I found myself a little corner to settle into. I looked over all the people jammed into the space. They were soaked, but every wet head had a broad grin. People were embracing each other and patting each other on the back. Some people had their phones out taking pictures and some taking videos. It didn't take long before a pungent odor filled the hallway. In a state where recreational marijuana is legal, I was surprised it took that long. The room was buzzing with conversations about the crazy weather. More were blown away by Steve Winwood's soon-to-be legendary performance. They were all truly happy. They all came hoping to get a glimpse of the spirit of rock 'n' roll. It was not just a glimpse. It was a full immersion as if on Max Yasgur's farm forty-five years earlier at Woodstock. (Right down to soaked underwear.)

The same security guy came back shouting that all was clear forty-five minutes later. When I found my seat again, they just about had the stage in some sort of working order. Steve was still pumped up from earlier. He sat at the keyboards and broke out an old Traffic tune, "The Low Spark of High Heeled Boys," causing Red Rocks to erupt. The set was abbreviated because of the delay. Intermission was a bit surreal as you watched the staff trying to remove three inches of hail using snow shovels. I was able to buy a cup of expensive bitter coffee. I drank it black and it warmed my insides and my hands. By the time the intermission ended the sky was clear and the stars shone bright. The temperature rebounded just enough to be considered pleasant.

Steely Dan is a big band with two permanent members. The first guy is the guitar player and songwriter named Walter Becker. He is sixty-six but looks eighty-six. He is a survivor whose drug binges were legendary. Donald Fagen is the other guy and the keyboard player. Many people think Donald's jazzy soul is the driving force in the band. The rest of the players work at the pleasure of these two guys. Steely Dan can be described as a jazz rock band with dabs of funk and R&B.

The band took the stage and the mood was a bit apprehensive at first. They walked into the situation of the evening with only second-hand information. Everyone else was working off of a firsthand wild evening of rock 'n' roll. It took a bit for the band to catch on. The energy of the evening was undeniable. The old ghosts that reside at Red Rocks were eventually stirred. Ten thousand rocking chair rockers were dancing and singing along with the band. By the time the band got to their song, "My Old School," there were ten thousand card-carrying AARP members sweating, shaking ass, and rocking out. It wasn't pretty, but it was heartfelt. It was old school. The survivors were at their best.

In my day, the encore was induced by the lighting of disposable lighters. Now it is from the flashlight option on a cell phone. After a stirring rendition of "Pretzel Logic," it was over. The concert, the trip, and my escape from the rat race. I eventually found my way down the mountain, into the car, and back to the hotel room. I finally turned on the television to look at the Weather Channel. There, on national television, was footage from Red Rocks. It was the most exciting weather event on the planet that evening. That was cool.

I sat in my hotel room trying to make sense of the week I stole away from the system. I never got to hear "Deacon Blues," but that was all right. I've seen the song before and will again. I thought about legendary fortuitous winds of nautical lore. Most associate it with blue skies and warming sunshine when a gentle breeze will fill sails taking sailors to where they needed to be. I thought about how they didn't need to be sunshine and lollipops. In fact, my fortuitous winds blew in on dark clouds and angry skies. Perhaps my ship needed to move on in a more expedited fashion. Sometimes you just have to trust the fates.

An Autumn Day

Once upon an Autumn day,
Colorful leaves began to fade
In the mist of Chilly, frosty air
As multitude of tree grew steadily bare.

—*Joseph T. Renaldi*

Life, when lived properly, mirrors good poetry. As the years stack up like cordwood, I begin to feel the prose that concerns itself with autumn in a personal way. The withering of the flow of life that runs fast and hard in our youth slows and life becomes deliberate. I look back and see myself in the memories of my parents. As I look at my parents, I see the foreshadowing of my fate. There is nothing warm or sexy in the effects of days passing upon their faces. A certain angst burrows into the center of my soul knowing their fate waits for me. If there is any comfort that can be grasped from the ongoing march into winter, it is that it is fair and uniform. That the weight of the years bends all backs without prejudice.

That seems a little melancholy, but if you can resist looking forward and can concentrate on the fall that befalls us presently, there is a golden hue. The hue of autumn. I have become a compilation of the life I have led. I wear the face I have earned. As I look in the mirror and assess the lines that the years have carved upon me I realize personal wisdom. Like the season, the fruits of my spring and summer are ripening to fruition. In proportion, the fading of my youth, the tasks at hand develop an ease that comes when wisdom replaces brute force and sheer will. I look at the compilations I have created. Some out of necessity and others from my heart. Some I share with the loves of my life. Some I love in a selfishness. A selfish solitude. If in the only reason that it has an intrinsic meaning that I would not know how to begin to explain.

One of the things I hang onto in that solitude is my time in the outdoors. It has become so personal that the best I can do is share the essence. To tell the story in such a way that it sparks a light. A light that is both familiar and comforting. To tell a tale that invokes a familiarity and brings a commonality that is both touching and warm. That inspires us to live and recount the things that bring out the fine details of our humanity.

In my life, I have found that a quiet fall day spent alone in nature carries these kinds of inspirations. I choose to go outside and camouflage my being along water, to walk alone and deliberately with a fly rod in my hand. Many years earlier I had purchased a beautiful bamboo fly rod at a yard sale that I stumbled upon. It was before money mattered much to me. I didn't have any so it was a balanced way of doing things. When I picked up the rod I immediately felt the love of a craftsman. The feeling that only an artist can impart to the object of art. Isn't that what artist do? The rod spoke to me. I had admired rods before but this was different. It was obvious that it was forgotten for years. The feeling the artist imparted into the work had gone unfelt and unappreciated. That made me want it so much more. I had ten dollars in my pocket. The seller wanted more. In the end, she was happy to take all I had. I took the rod home and cleaned it carefully. I fished it very hard over the next several years. It fit me well. It wasn't until some other flyfisherman pointed out that I shouldn't be fishing that rod. It turned out that the rod had a collector's value that easily exceeded my net worth at the time by several folds.

There are some who would have been overjoyed by the news. It was a solid and stunning slap in the face. It was like being told that you were not supposed to love the girl from the other side of the tracks. I began to research the rod and in doing so I understood why I had fallen so hard for the piece of art. It was older than I had imagined. Its medium action made catching anything beautiful fun. It took many more years to understand how rare beautiful fun is. It was just another facet of the art of the piece.

Eventually, time allowed me to understand the meaning of balance. That I needed to understand the responsibility I had to the rod and myself. That I didn't own the rod but instead was its current caretaker. It was through these pangs of responsibility that I came up with a working arrangement with myself on behalf of the trust with the fly rod. I would fish the rod every fall. It would be a way to mark the years as they passed. Some people notched a headboard, prisoners tallied them on the wall, I fished my Payne fly rod alone in joyful contemplation every fall. In the process of doing so, I examine my life.

Behind my house is a pair of ponds created by my neighbors as a suitable alternative to ugly catch basins. They were landscaped and filled with koi. Water is the substance that drives life and these ponds are no different. The ponds went wild in the middle of suburbia in the same way that moss grows between the cracks of a sidewalk. In the spring, frogs and toads would awaken and serenade me in high-pitched choirs. The summer would dance around the small ponds' reflections. Waterfowl would raise their families, tadpoles would grow legs, the koi would sun under the surface with their backbones breaking the tension of the water.

The activity would build itself into a crescendo somewhere around the Fourth of July. After that it would gradually wind down. Each evening while tending my garden, I would encounter my amphibious insect control. Toads relish my garden and I let them. As the summer waned into the start of fall, my toads seem to diminish. Then one day I notice they are all gone. Their departure is better than any science for forecasting the coming winter.

It was this year, at toad-out time, I realized that things were getting by me. One of the things was that I had not yet fished the Payne rod. I had not assessed this fifty-third year. It might not seem that important at first glance. I am not sure how it got by me. Too many distractions? Are my wits dulling around the edges? Whatever the root cause, I was not paying close enough attention.

Tradition and spiritual contemplation are important fibers to our humanity. Usually important, I would take time to go to some isolated pretty spot in the Catskills or Adirondacks, or occasionally the Alleghanys. We are blessed with three beautiful and ancient mountain ranges in New York. Ancient mountains carry the spirituality of ancient wisdom. Younger, newer mountains such as the Rocky Mountains are considered challenged when it comes to the wisdom of the universe.

I realized I was almost out of time if I was to preserve this annual rite of self-contemplation. I would have to forgo the luxury of a planned trip to some hidden gem of nature. I would have to search the compilation of places that I had inventoried over the years. There were many local streams filled with the annual runs of salmonids from the Great Lakes. Big steelhead and brown trout were fulfilling old yearnings in many of the tributaries that lined the south shore of Lake Ontario. My old Payne bamboo fly rod was never built for such big, strong fish. I would have to dig deeper in my repertoire of places. In wandering through the spots of my life, I focused on one. It was a pretty stream I found many years ago. When I first glanced her many years ago, I fell in love.

Her water ran clean and clear. Her bottom was classic slate with long riffles pouring into picturesque pools. When I finally managed to place a fly upon her waters I was given a surprise in the form of smallmouth bass. The one thing I could not see from afar was that her waters ran too warm for trout.

If a river is to be void of trout, the best consolation prize is smallmouth bass. They eagerly smashed poppers. They fought with a stout heart and would tail walk at the slightest provocation. If an engineer were to sit at his drafting table and create the perfect fish for fly fishing, it would come out looking a lot like the smallmouth bass. The more I prayed over it, the more I liked the idea of going to that spot for my annual review of life.

I started to recall the first time I fished her. Ronald Reagan was president and his wife Nancy was telling us "Just Say No!" Our psyches were formed around the fear of the Cold War, where the security of the era was based upon an absurd principle of mutually-assured destruction. The fragile balance of which was illuminated by the Cuban missile crisis and Nikita Khrushchev banging his shoe on a table in a big building in New York.

Of course, each generation has its hardships. My grandfather would recall the harshness of the Great Depression. "We would walk to school uphill through ten feet of snow, both ways!' looking around to make sure we were listening. "Then we would come home to a supper of stone stew!" If one of his cronies was around, he would chime in, "You had stones? You're a lucky bastard, all we had was dirt!" If a third was present, you would hear, "Dirt? Oh, you lucky son of a bitch, we could only have dirt on Christmas!"

If someone was around from the generation before, you would hear how he only received half an orange and a broken bottle for Christmas and was glad of it. The current generation coming up is the one with real troubles. We are handing them a country where the American Dream is on life support and the planet is severely damaged.

It was a long time ago when I first fished that water.

In that time, the stream was situated in what was considered rural. It ran in the back of a dairy pasture. To be more accurate, it ran behind a bull pasture. One of the interesting things was to figure out how to cross the pasture without getting gored. The bull that ruled that pasture during that time was big and perpetually pissed. To fish the water, you would have to endure the scaled-down version of running with the bulls in Pamploma. I could easily recall a time when I mistimed my start. In the end, it was a close affair with me tossing my bag and rod over the fence while simultaneously I slid under the barbed wire. It was not a clean getaway. The barbed wire shredded my jeans and I still carry a slight scar all these years later. I did love that animal. He was an effective stream-keeper. Very few were willing to run with him just to cast a fly.

All these years later, the bull is gone, the dairy farm is gone, and the rural little town has grown into an upscale bedroom community. The pasture that my bull once guarded is now occupied by a wealthy housing tract. The homes there are well above my pay grade. It is the kind of place where you purchase the lot and the builder has a dozen or so blueprints approved for those lots. Most of the lots have been sold. With the slowdown in housing, two lots remain open. It is like a mouth with a couple of teeth missing. I will be able to access my stream via those empty lots. In realizing that a time may come, sooner than later, that those lots will be built on, my chest tightened. My repertoire of fishing spots has suffered over the years. I am glad that I could grow up when there was more rural land than settled tracts.

The late fall hours of light lessened more dramatically every day. I had gotten a start that was later than was prudent. It meant I had a few hours to meet my self-imposed obligation. As I approached the stream, I looked for any cues that might help me find a way to fool my quarry. Insects were almost non-existent.

I did notice a few black and orange beetles sporadically floating upon the water. I tied on a small popper with similar colors. I was able to lay down a pretty cast. Working the water correctly. Placing my bug against boulders all along the slack flow that late-fall conditions gave the stream.

In a couple hours of fishing, all I could manage was one small ten-inch bass. It was fun. It was beautiful. It was slow. There are those who say that the best part of fishing isn't in the catching. I know what they mean but the intent does work better when the catching is good. The sun overhead was past its apex. I knew where there was a good spot a couple miles downstream. I would have to pick up the pace if I wanted to have any time to spend there.

This stream had some typical features of a Northeastern stream. It was boulder-strewn and the rocks under the surface had a coating of slick, slippery weed and algae. You had to be careful. I spent many years moving over that kind of terrain. Hopping, jumping, and balancing along in a forward direction. Over the years, it became second nature. I always found that kind of loco-motion amazing. That the human brain could make all the calcu-lations and transmit the precise movement of feet, legs, and body. Multiple figuring of distance and geometry, force, and accelera-tion, all within fractions of seconds.

I had done this many times. Occasionally the machine makes a miscalculation and I fall. On this day, I had one of those errors and fell hard. "Oh shit!" I remember thinking on my way down. It's funny those are the words that come to mind when the machine fails. I fell hard. I didn't bounce back up like I did in my youth. I laid in the water. My brain was working out a new problem. It was assessing damage. My cotton shirt was acting like a wick. Cold water was travelling up the cotton and soaking my back and ass. The back of my head laying shallow in the chilly water with my eyes staring up at the sky.

It was this moment that I decided to fulfill my yearly tradition. What the fuck. While I was assessing bodily damage, I might as well assess the previous year. I looked for my fly rod. It was still in my right hand sticking straight up in the air. Somewhere in my subconscious extra calculations were made on behalf of the rod. "Oh God," I thought, "How fucked up am I?" Then I started to laugh. I placed the wellness of that bamboo rod over various body parts. I noticed that the sun seemed to have a dullness to it. Fall days can be like that. I was thinking that I was like that too. I knew, too, that nothing was wrong with my brain's calculations. It was my body's inability to react to the directions it was sent. I was feeling like this late fall day. I kept looking at the sky through branches without leaves. My mind drifted to a girl I loved in high school. I just found out a couple of days earlier that she had passed. How years earlier, in a place very close to this stream, we shared a love embrace. Never once giving thought to this moment. I developed a lump in my throat. I felt like life was winding down like a calliope.

I have a perverse side to me. I started to tell myself that if I didn't break my ass, it might be a good idea to get up. I finished the damage assessment and decided that I might have some big throbbing bruises but might get away with just that. I did manage to get to my feet. I tore a hole at the elbow of my shirt. I tore a hole in my elbow. It was bleeding but starting to clot. Finally, I found a hole in the ass of my waders. I would patch it. It would join the others. Each was a badge of honor.

I gathered my consciousness and bruised, chilled body and went on to the spot I was thinking about. It was the site of an old grist mill. The mill was long gone but enough of the dam existed to create a large pool strewn with big boulders and five feet of water. It was always kind enough to hold several large bass. There was not much fishing time left. I did manage to get comfortable and as if a present from the fishing gods, my casts were pretty.

They were rewarded with several large rock bass. A couple of them pushed an honest two pounds. I found myself with a broad smile. It reminded me of an old joke. What does a fat chick and a moped have in common? They are both fun as hell to ride until one of your friends sees you. (My apologies to mopeds and fat chicks. The joke is a bit politically incorrect. Like all humor, it is about the exaggeration of some truth.) Now you can add catching giant rock bass with a bamboo Payne rod to the moped and the slightly overweight girl.

The sun was getting low and I was getting stiff. I did hurt myself. I was sore, and the cold dampness was setting into my bones. I suddenly wanted to be home and dry. It would be a couple of hours before I was home, showered, and sitting in front of a roaring fire. I had a chance to do some thinking. I was sitting in the middle of my beautiful library full of my collection of leather-bound books. They all were clad in 24-carat gold. It struck me that I could have never been able to do that in my youth. In fact, I was getting ready to reread Jack Kerouac's *On the Road*. The thing about great literature is that you can reread in various stages of life and get entirely new perspectives from the work. I held the stately brown leather-bound Easton press volume in my hand. I was soaking the warmth from the fire and it felt so good chasing the chill out of my bones. It occurred to me that style was one way to offset the loss of youth. Sometimes small epiphanies are just what the doctor ordered. A little planning and a little style would work in the coming Autumns. Next year I will take the Payne and fish for some fat brook trout in the Adirondacks or maybe some scrappy cutthroat somewhere in Colorado. The real trick will be to fill the time from here to there in kind. I would be okay with, "He may be getting old but the man has style!"